The Liberal Record

The Liberal Record

How Liberals Changed the World

Marcelo Brazzi

Copyright © 2019 by Marcelo Brazzi.

Library of Congress Control Number:	2019906833
ISBN: Hardcover	978-1-7960-3515-5
Softcover	978-1-7960-3514-8
eBook	978-1-7960-3513-1

All rights reserved. No part of this book may be reproduced or transmitted in any form or by any means, electronic or mechanical, including photocopying, recording, or by any information storage and retrieval system, without permission in writing from the copyright owner.

The views expressed in this work are solely those of the author and do not necessarily reflect the views of the publisher, and the publisher hereby disclaims any responsibility for them.

Scripture quotations marked NIV are taken from the Holy Bible, New International Version®. NIV®. Copyright © 1973, 1978, 1984 by International Bible Society. Used by permission of Zondervan. All rights reserved. [Biblica]

Any people depicted in stock imagery provided by Getty Images are models, and such images are being used for illustrative purposes only.
Certain stock imagery © Getty Images.

Print information available on the last page.

Rev. date: 03/10/2020

To order additional copies of this book, contact:
Xlibris
1-888-795-4274
www.Xlibris.com
Orders@Xlibris.com
793077

CONTENTS

Prologue xv
Acknowledgment xvii
Introduction xix

Part 1: The Great Political Divide 1
   Definitions 1
      Summary 6
   The Great Change 6
      Fairness Doctrine 7
      Repeal of Fairness 7
      Credibility 8
      Dunning-Kruger Effect 12

Part 2: Background 13
   The Beginning 13
   Ancient Democracies—Greece 14
   Ancient Democracies—Rome 17
   Magna Carta Libertatum 18
   Four Quantum Leaps 19
      Language 20
      Writing 20
   The Information Revolutions 22
      Printing 22
      Radio Frequency Transmission 24

Part 3: The First Law of Politics 26
Independence 26
Slavery 30
    Cause of the Civil War 32
    The 1861 Texas Articles of Secession 33
    The 1861 Georgia Articles of Secession 34
Women Voting 37
Worker's Rights 39
Health Care 41
Prostitution 43
Prudes and Nudes 45
Illegal Drugs 46
    War on Drugs 47

Part 4: American Exceptionalism 50
Weights and Measures 51
Temperature 53
Time 54
Sports 55
    Soccer 55
    Football 56
    Baseball and Basketball 59
Health Care 59
    Competition 60
    Profits 62
    Overhead 64
    Other Problems 65
Handguns 67
    Public Opinion 68

Part 5: Beyond the Headlines 73
Democrat and Republican Economies 73
    Regulations 78
    Removing Consumer Protections 80
    Economic Evolution 81

    Rise and Fall of Communism 82
    Rise and Fall of Unregulated Capitalism 83
    Trickle Down 86
    Minimum Wage 90
    The Working Class 91
Abortion 95
Global Warming 98
    Leaded Gas 99
    Ford Pinto 100
    Cigarette Cancer 101
    Acid Rain 103
    Climate Scientists 103
    The Great Hoax Conspiracy 104
    The Science 104
    Denial 105
    Consequences 106
Democrats Must Go on the Offense 111
Personalities 114
Opinions vs. Facts 115
Voter Fraud 117
    Voting Problems 119
    Conservative Disinformation Campaigns 120
Small Government 122
Trump 123

Part 6: Beyond the Horizon 127
Automation 128
Population Policies 129
Permanent Political Divide 134
    Social Networks 135
    A Divided Country 136
    The United Alliance 137

Epilogue	141
Appendix	143
Everything You Need to Know	143
The Laws of Politics	143
Republicans Oppose Teaching Critical Thinking	144
Dictionary Definitions	144
Cognitive Dissonance	144
Dunning-Kruger Effect	144
Liberal	145
Conservative	145
Major Accomplishments of Social Liberals	147
The Conservatives' Record	149
Republican Filibusters Blocking Obama Recovery Bills	149
Major Republican Lies	151
Famous Quotes by Trump	157
Must-See References	159
Videos	159
Books	159
References	165
Index	173

TABLE

Table 1: Dictionary Definitions 4
Table 2: Major Accomplishments of Liberals....................................5
Table 3: International Drug Prices 61
Table 4: 2017 Health-Care CEO Compensation............................63
Table 5: Health Care Quality of Service by Country 65
Table 6: Income Equality by Country—GINI Index.....................85
Table 7: Types of Pregnancy Failures 96
Table 8: Global Warming Components 105
Table 9: Criminal Activity by Party 114
Table 10: Strange Things Republicans Continue to Believe 117

CHART

Chart 1:   Audience Knowledge by Media 10
Chart 2:   Opinions vs. Facts 11
Chart 3:   Number of Guns vs. Number of Gun Deaths 69
Chart 4:   Gun Deaths by Country 70
Chart 5:   GDP Growth by Party 76
Chart 6:   Job Growth by Party 77
Chart 7:   Decline in Unions, Decline in Wages 93
Chart 8:   Decline in Union Membership 94
Chart 9:   Greenhouse Gas Accumulation 109
Chart 10: Sea Level Rise 110
Chart 11: World Population History 132
Chart 12: Life Expectancy 133
Chart 13: Happiness Rankings of Countries 152
Chart 14: GINI Income Equality by Country 153
Chart 15: S&P 500 by President 154
Chart 16: Indictments and Convictions by Administration 155
Chart 17: Federal Aid by State 160
Chart 18: Gun-Death Rate 161
Chart 19: Obesity by State 162
Chart 20: Heart Failures by State 163
Chart 21: Median Household Income 164

This work is dedicated to the late great fiction writer George Snyder. George was my guide and friend, who always gave me encouragement, advice, and ideas.

Every nation gets the government it deserves.
—Joseph de Maistre

PROLOGUE

It is safe to say world history before the twentieth century is not well-known. There seems to be little appreciation of how we have progressed from the world of illiteracy to the magical world of DNA, democracy, and drive-through wedding chapels. The historical record is one of humans constantly seeking to improve their freedoms, their standard of living, and true justice.

The leaders of this intellectual and cultural revolution were explorers, scientists, writers, entrepreneurs, and social liberals. For the past 400 years, humanity has been on a slow but relentless migration from the old conservative world of kings and slaves to a world of liberties and popular rule. This book sheds light on how we got here. Unbiased sources are referenced throughout the book.

When deciding whom we will vote for, we tend to focus on the individual candidates. We judge their character, their sincerity, their passion, and their positions against our personal hot topics. We often dismiss the party affiliations as only minor concerns. But the most significant decisions are made by the entire party and not by the individual. Things like lifetime judicial appointments, gun laws, and health care are determined by majority votes in Congress. In today's political environment, important votes are usually split along party lines. So the party affiliations of candidates are crucial. This book explores the history and differences between political parties.

As used here, *American* refers to "people of the United States" unless otherwise specified. This is technically inaccurate since *American* refers to "anyone living in either of the two American continents." A Canadian is from Canada. A Mexican is from Mexico. We have no word to describe people of the United States, so we default back to using *American* for lack of a better word.

The author here is a card-carrying independent who voted for Jack Kennedy, Ronald Reagan, George H. W. Bush, and Bill Clinton.

ACKNOWLEDGMENT

I am indebted to my son Mical, who kept me focused on solid ideas and clarifications.

INTRODUCTION

Stop listening to the bombastic loudmouths on the radio and television and the internet. To hell with them. They don't want anything done for the public good.

—Senator John McCain

This book is not about fiscal conservatives and fiscal liberals. This book is primarily about social conservatives and social liberals. This may seem like an unnecessary distinction. Most people today think of *conservative* and *republican* as virtual synonyms. The same is true of the words *liberal* and *democrat*. However, in the past, these philosophies did not fit tidily and distinctly into partisan identities.

Social liberals are the focus of this book; however, there are issues tied to political parties, so political parties are mentioned in those cases.

In the 1800s, some issues were the opposite of the partisan associations as we know them today. The Republican Party was founded in 1854 as the party of liberals in opposition to conservatives of the slave-holding Southern states. The Democrat Party was split between liberals in the Northern states and conservatives in the Southern states. Southern conservatives used to be Democrats (Dixiecrats), but in the second half of the twentieth century, they changed their allegiance to the Republican Party.

When today's Republicans claim credit for the abolition of slavery, they are omitting the most critical distinction—in 1860, Republicans were liberals, while today, Republicans are social conservatives. A social liberal in 1860 would be a social liberal in 1960, but not in the same political party.

When removed from partisan context, there is a lot of agreement on most issues. Capitalism is embraced by all Americans, no matter what some radio agitators want you to believe. Efficient and effective government operations are sought by everyone in spite of attempts to make this a wedge issue. Background checks of gun buyers are desired by everyone, including staunch gun-rights groups regardless of party affiliation. Same-sex marriage, Obamacare, and cannabis possession are no longer divisive issues with the vast majority of Americans. As a group, Americans are really not that much different from one another. However, a great deal of effort has been dedicated to creating differences and exaggerating them for partisan reasons. One technique employed is to redefine the meanings of basic English words. For example, Rush Limbaugh wants you to hate liberals, so he said on the radio, "[Liberals] think parents and grandparents are worthless"[1]. Without the least bit of evidence, Limbaugh also said, "Your kids are being indoctrinated into cults of left-wing radicalism. There is no slight area of commonality where we can compromise or agree. They are entirely different from us"[2]. Unfortunately, many Americans actually believe such incredible disinformation. This develops an undeserved, intense hatred of liberals that makes all other disinformation easily believed, no matter how irrational or illogical.

This redefinition campaign has been successful. Much of the public no longer knows what the words *conservative* and *liberal* mean. All they know is what they hear on biased talk radio or TV, which has no interest in being accurate or objective.

PART ONE
The Great Political Divide

A Conservative is a fellow who is standing athwart history yelling 'Stop!'
—William F. Buckley Jr.

There have always been different beliefs and policies in politics. But over the past few decades, the differences have become extremely polarized. This is not normal, and it needs to be understood.

Definitions

In the discussion of any controversial issue, it is necessary that there is agreement on the definitions of common English words.[3] Table 1 presents dictionary definitions of the terms *conservative* and *liberal*. Without a clear understanding of basic English words, neither side of an issue is able to communicate accurately with the other side. Many social conservatives will describe liberals with words like *communist*, *hate America*, *lazy scum*, along with a string of profanities.

Of course, that is absurd and promoted strictly to get voters to hate social liberals. False ideas like this are common and successful because many voters are inclined to believe whatever they hear. They assume that if they heard it on the TV, it must be true. This book was written partly to encourage voters to be open-minded and to be fully aware of both sides of all issues.

Some people argue that times have changed and these traditional definitions no longer apply. This is a false argument. People in general have not changed. We all want security, stability, peace, and prosperity today—the same as what people in the past have always wanted. The words *conservative* and *liberal* exist in languages around the world. It makes no sense for some political person to attempt to redefine words only in the USA for his own political propaganda purposes. If they were different only in the USA, language translators would go crazy trying to translate American English into Romanian or even to British English.

Words change over time, but they never flip over to mean something completely different. When they change, it is through colloquial usage and not by the edict of political activists. The reader is cautioned to bear in mind that parties and philosophies can, and do, change over time. But it is virtually impossible for the basic English words in table 1 to change their meaning.

Physiological studies have shown that there are deep physical and psychological differences between social liberals and social conservatives[4]. Many studies have been conducted in this area of science. It has been determined that the right amygdala of the brain is larger and more active in social conservatives. This part of the brain is associated with, among other things, fear. Other studies have established a correlation between the DRD4 (dopamine receptor D4) gene[5] and conservative views. Conservatives have physical differences from liberals that cause them to have higher levels of fear, anxiety, hatred, and distrust. In addition to this, an individual's life experiences can also contribute to their sense of fear or distrust of others.

This is reflected in the conservatives' fear of anything or anyone that is different. They do not trust new policies and programs such as Social Security and the Affordable Care Act. This explains why conservatives always want a bigger military. They also tend to believe anyone of a different ethnicity is a threat to them.

These feelings are often justified by assuming a rare, isolated incident is a common, daily occurrence. Conservatives have always opposed all social progress. See table 2. Conservative politicians and right-wing media play to the natural fears and anxieties of conservatives.

There are misconceptions among the general public regarding liberals and conservatives. Table 2 summarizes some key liberal accomplishments in US history. These items were opposed by conservatives.

Table 1
Dictionary Definitions

Conservative [k*uh* n-**sur**-v*uh*-tiv] adjective

1. Disposed to preserve existing conditions, institutions, etc. or to restore traditional ones and to limit change.
2. Cautiously moderate or purposefully low: a conservative estimate.
3. Traditional in style or manner, avoiding novelty or showiness: a conservative suit.
4. Of or relating to the Conservative Party.
5. Having the power or tendency to conserve or preserve.

Liberal [**lib**-er-*uh* l, **lib**-r*uh* l] adjective

1. Favorable to progress or reform, as in political or religious affairs.
2. Noting or pertaining to a political party advocating measures of progressive political reform.
3. Pertaining to, based on, or advocating liberalism, especially the freedom of the individual and government guarantees of individual rights and liberties.
4. Favorable to or in accord with concepts of maximum individual freedom possible, especially as guaranteed by law and secured by governmental protection of civil liberties.
5. Favoring or permitting freedom of action, especially with respect to matters of personal belief or expression: *a liberal policy toward dissident artists and writers.*
6. Relating to representational forms of government rather than aristocracies and monarchies.
7. Free from prejudice or bigotry; tolerant: *liberal attitude toward foreigners*

Table 2
Major Accomplishments of Liberals

- Women's right to vote
- Freedom to sell alcohol (after it was outlawed)
- Public education for everyone
- Fairness in broadcasting (1949–1987)
- Declaration of independence from Britain
- Separation of church and state
- Child labor outlawed
- Emancipation Proclamation—end of slavery
- Medicare
- Freedom of same-sex marriages
- Social Security
- Monopolies outlawed
- Freedom to use marijuana
- 1957 Civil Rights Act
- Affordable Care Act
- Worker-management agreements
    - Forty-hour workweek
    - Living wages
    - Employer health insurance
    - Work breaks
    - Extra pay for overtime hours
    - Equal opportunity for all races, genders, ethnicities
    - Protection from sexual harassment and inequality
    - Pension plans
    - Termination and discipline justification procedures
    - Paid vacations
    - Workers' rights
- Consumer protections from dangerous products
    - Safe food and drugs—FDA
    - Seat belts, catalytic converters, airbags
    - Potable water and breathable air—EPA
    - Consumer financial protections—CFPB

Summary

Liberals are the agents of change and progress, particularly in shifting power to the general citizenry.

Conservatives resist changes and anything or anyone new or different. That's why they are called conservatives.

Liberals have been behind all progress that has changed humanity from the world of kings and slaves to the world of freedoms and democracy, which we enjoy today.

Virtually everything we take for granted today in our government and culture is the result of liberal progress over the years.

The Great Change

After World War II, the world discovered what had really been going on inside Germany before and during the war. The world was horrified at the discovery of all the mass graves and gas chambers. The millions of bodies were not combatants but everyone, including thousands of women and children. Details were learned of how Hitler came to power without ever having the support of the majority of the German people. Hitler never won an election. (It is also possible to become a US president without getting the most votes). With a combination of events and constant propaganda fueling the fears, hatred, and frustrations of the working class, Hitler was appointed chancellor in 1930, and he then arranged to become the führer in 1934. One of the keys to Hitler's rise was his use of radios and newspapers to flood the land with unchallenged political hate speech.

This information got Americans asking themselves, Is it possible for that to happen here? Then they would all laugh and say, "Don't be ridiculous. Americans would never fall for all that Nazi hatemongering." Someone in the back of the room shouted out, "Yeah, but it's better to be safe than sorry. Let's do something to make sure that can't happen here."

Fairness Doctrine

So the fairness doctrine was implemented in 1949. This doctrine required that TV and radio audiences be given a diversity of viewpoints on all issues. This law did not violate the First Amendment of the US Constitution, which guarantees the freedom of speech because it did not prohibit speech but rather required that opinionated broadcast must be fairly balanced with opposing opinions. For example, Republican senator Joe McCarthy of Wisconsin was free to lie on NBC that Hollywood was controlled by dozens of communists. But NBC was required to provide equal time to a Hollywood executive to refute the charges and demand that McCarthy provide proof of his charges. Eventually McCarthy was condemned (not censured) in 1954 by a Senate vote of 67–22. He was essentially ostracized socially and politically from that point on.

Thanks to the fairness doctrine, the political spectrum was fairly balanced among liberals, conservatives, and moderates. There have always been people on the extreme right and left, but this fringe element was relatively small and was considered to be irrational and out of touch with what was really happening in the country.

Conservative Republicans continuously opposed the fairness in broadcasting regulation. The fairness doctrine made it difficult for Republicans to select and manipulate the public into believing only what they wanted them to believe. This is precisely what the doctrine was designed to prevent. Republicans continued to attack and resist the fairness doctrine long after it was established.

Repeal of Fairness

In 1981, Ronald Reagan was elected president and the Republicans finally got what they had been fighting for. In 1987, Reagan repealed the TV and radio fairness doctrine, and that was the end of the traditional cooperative, compromising form of government we had enjoyed for the last 200 years. America had never been the same since that tragic event.

A few weeks after fairness was repealed, Rush Limbaugh, with this new release from accountability, cheerfully plugged in his radio microphone. Fox News soon followed Limbaugh. Instead of repealing the fairness law, it should have been expanded to include cable and satellite transmissions. These conservative outlets proceeded to become 24-hour propaganda programs demonizing Democrats. They were free from any accountability or even ethical practices. Joe McCarthy types were free to make all kinds of false charges without having to worry about fairness or even common decency and ethics.

Fox News, Rush Limbaugh, Alex Jones, and their accomplices had only one objective, and that was to create as much fear and hatred of the liberals as they could through any means possible. They did not present complete, accurate information from both sides of issues. Instead, they presented only one distorted side with maximum partisan spin. This was exactly what the fairness regulation had prohibited.

The Republican's repeal of fairness and the constant, irresponsible political propaganda created extremists with irrational hatred of Democrats. In 2018, one of these hate-filled extremists sent 14 bombs to popular Democrat leaders. Fortunately, none of the bombs exploded. This is one example of why Conservatives should not have repealed the fairness regulation.

Revival of the fairness doctrine, or some version of it, had been discussed and proposed by Democrats several times, but at this time, the US has no limits on one-sided political broadcasting.

The fact that conservatives repealed fairness and liberals fought to keep it tells you everything you need to know about conservatives and liberals.

Credibility

There have been many studies and fact-checks by independent, objective institutions over the years to define the levels of credibility for the various programs and networks. Every one of the unbiased studies reported that conservative Fox News was the least credible of all the information providers. The far right would claim all those studies were biased; they were not. They opened all their data, procedures, and analysis for review and critique. But the far right did not care about that. They made their charges of bias no matter what the reality was.

The Project on Excellence in Journalism report showed that 68 % of Fox cable stories contained personal opinions as compared to MSNBC at 27% and CNN at 4%.[6] The "Content Analysis" portion of their 2005 report also concluded that "Fox was measurably more one-sided than the other networks, and Fox journalists were more opinionated on the air."

Chart 1
Audience Knowledge by Media

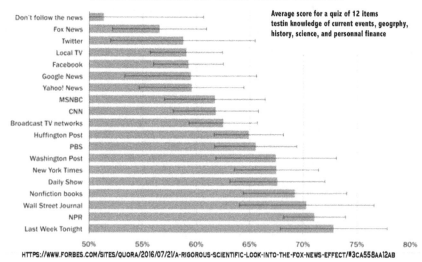

Source
https://www.businessinsider.com/study-watching-fox-news-makes-you-less-informed-than-watching-no-news-at-all-2012-5[(7)]

Chart 2
Opinions vs. Facts

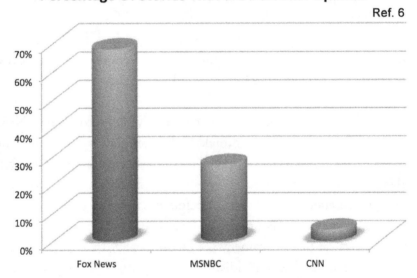

Source: https://en.wikipedia.org/wiki/Fox_News_controversies#Content_analysis_studies (6)

A few of the many studies regarding media credibility are the following:
- A Scientific Look into "Fox News Effect" [6]
- Watching Only Fox News Makes You Less Informed Than Watching No News at All [7]
- Fox News Misleading 72% of the Time [8]

Dunning-Kruger Effect

The Dunning-Kruger effect is a psychological phenomenon of illusory superiority. "The Dunning-Kruger effect is a cognitive bias in which people of low ability have illusory superiority and mistakenly assess their cognitive ability as greater than it is"[9].

It was identified as a form of cognitive bias in Kruger and Dunning's 1999 study, "Unskilled and Unaware of It: How Difficulties in Recognizing One's Own Incompetence Lead to Inflated Self-Assessments".

The Dunning-Kruger effect is commonly observed in Fox News viewers. They are given minimal, highly selected information and misinformation that viewers believe is complete and accurate. Viewers believe they have better information than everyone else. But every Fox News presentation is highly edited before broadcast to cultivate hatred and distrust of liberals. For example, Jeanine Pirro of Fox News screams "Demon rats" at the TV cameras. No traditional channels like ABC or NBC have ever used such childish playground attacks on any parties or individuals. The Fox News policy of using such silly, slanderous name-calling is proof that the goal of Fox News is not to accurately report issues and events but to create negative feelings about Democrats. Fox News has continued this campaign of misinformation and propaganda because it works. Viewers believe whatever they hear on Fox News and think everything else must be wrong. When Fox News accused Hillary Clinton of corruption their audience believed it without any actual evidence.

False and biased information is the biggest threat to democracy, to freedom, and to the USA. This is the reason that the fairness doctrine was established in 1949.

PART TWO

Background

Were it left to me to decide whether we should have a government without newspapers or newspapers without a government, I should not hesitate a moment to prefer the latter.

—Thomas Jefferson

The concepts of conservative and liberal did not always exist. Part two looks back over time to set the stage for the eventual development of social conservatives and social liberals.

The Beginning

There is evidence of hominids living on Earth over 7 million years ago. That length of time is nearly impossible for us to comprehend. We cannot conceptualize numbers that contain more than about four- or five-decimal characters. However, of those 7 million years, the hominid species, *Homo sapiens* (us), has existed for only about 180,000 years or 6,000 generations. That's a small enough number that theoretically you could trace your ancestors back to a cave woman in Ethiopia, East Africa. If you did and used a time machine to meet her, you would see she looked no different from anyone you might meet in a shopping mall today, minus the eye shadow and breast implants.

Virtually all those 6,000 generations lived short, painful lives of hard work, disease, filth, and stress. Other than the sun, fire was the only source of both heat and light. And the only doctors were witch doctors that could not cure anything but were happy to turn your favorite wife's secret lover into a lizard.

Anthropologists believed some consensus decision-making had existed at the tribal level since the caveman days. As tribes grew into communities, it became expeditious to have a single decision maker. It was estimated that the ability to speak evolved about 140,000 years ago, probably on a cloudy Tuesday in Tanzania. The next day, the first politician jumped up and said, "I will give everyone a shiny stone if you call me king and help me get rid of those annoying Neanderthals."

That structure of a single powerful man having all the power was the only form of government for thousands of years. People would follow whoever had the biggest club or whoever had the most wives. That period existed for 99% of the time humans and language have existed.

No one ever questioned the concept of monarchs, dictators, or emperors. It was just taken for granted. If some gang of thugs did not cut off your head, you would show your gratitude by occasionally giving them a bag of carrots and maybe throw in one of your daughters, usually the lazy one. The concepts of liberal, conservative, libertarian, and so forth were unheard of. However, some monarchs like Peter the Great and Julius Caesar had more empathy for the lower classes than most other kings had and treated all citizens with respect and considerations.

Ancient Democracies—Greece

About 2,400 years ago, the novel idea of all the men being directly involved in government was developed in each of the city-states of Greece. That was the first known exception to the universal paradigm of autocratic form of government.

In the sixth century BCE, a central national government did not exist in Greece. Each city had its own laws and leaders, although they had a sense of community with the other cities that shared their language, religion, and customs. There were groups of wealthy families in each Greek city-state that served as government. The reason a single powerful leader could not gain complete control was that the wealthy families could not coalesce around a single popular individual. Each group trusted none of the other groups.

The lower classes were not slaves, although they functioned in that capacity. These labor-class citizens endured physical and financial abuses by the top 1% who benefitted from all their hard work. These laborers toiled in the hot sun cutting the grass and shrubbery of the local cheese exporter, and all they got was a mangy old goat at the end of the month. They were also required to enroll in the army reserves and defend the city against local rebels and against Persian invaders. So in 507 BCE, when they met at the shopping mall on Saturday, they complained to one another. Someone said they should choose a spokesperson to demand a role in government. They drafted Cleisthenes, who was respected and trusted for his unbiased wisdom and fair treatment of all classes.

Cleisthenes was a gifted speaker who promoted the novel idea that all the citizens should be part of the governing process. Cleisthenes introduced a system of political reforms that he called *demokratia*, or "rule by the people." This system was comprised of three separate institutions: the *ekklesia*, a sovereign governing body that wrote laws and dictated foreign policy; the *boule*, a council of representatives from the ten Athenian tribes; and the *dikasteria*, the popular courts in which citizens argued cases before a group of lottery-selected jurors. Citizens did not vote for representatives but voted on the actual laws and proposals in large gatherings of 400 people. If we used this process in the USA today, we would have no senators or governors. We would all vote on proposed laws. This is actually done in some states, like California, that put propositions on ballots for everyone to vote on. Someday we may all vote on secure, encrypted internet sites.

This Greek democracy reached its zenith of advancements in art, culture, science, and architecture during the Golden Age of Pericles (449–431 BCE). Pericles was not the ruler but was respected by everyone as a great leader. Along with many other accomplishments, Pericles promoted the construction of the Parthenon on the Acropolis. The Parthenon pillars are still standing and are a major tourist attraction.

Pericles is considered to be the first great liberal leader. He is included in the pantheon of great liberal revolutionaries—Jefferson, Lincoln, Roosevelt, Luther, and perhaps the greatest liberal of all history, Jesus Christ.

The liberal Christ was able to get God to change many of his Old Testament policies. Before Christ, God was a vengeful, demanding entity with lists of sins (Leviticus 20:10) punishable by death. For example, "If *there is* a man who commits adultery with another man's wife, or who commits adultery with his friend's wife, the adulterer and the adulteress shall surely be put to death."

This pre-Christ god also considered polygamy to be the normal, accepted form of marriage. King David had eight recognized wives named Michal, Abigail, Bathsheba, Ahinoam, Maacah, Haggith, Abital, and Eglah (2 Samuel 3:2–5; 1 Chronicles 3:1–3). According to 2 Samuel 5:13, David married more wives in Jerusalem.

Christ convinced God to become more liberal and to convert into a loving, forgiving, merciful entity. God agreed to change, so he revised the many traditional laws including those on polygamy and extramarital sex. An influential spokesman of early Christians, Paul of Tarsus, rather than Christ, is recognized as having set the new rules for sex and marriage. People liked this new kind and forgiving version of God 2.0 and have been fighting religious wars ever since then.

Athenian democracy survived for two centuries. Greece then became a Roman province. Although ancient Rome ruled over Greece for many centuries, the Romans always acknowledged the Greeks to be the most educated, talented, and advanced of all cultures. The Romans adopted much of Greek religion, art, and architecture.

Ancient Democracies—Rome

Rome was founded in 753 BCE. Like all other civilizations at the time, it was established with a king as the ruler. This kingdom lasted for 244 years. In 509 BCE, the city-state of Rome overthrew the monarchy and a representative form of government was established. However, the upper-class patricians ran this republic. The lower-class plebeians had no say in the government. As it has been throughout history, the army consisted mostly of lower-class men. The plebs were not dummies and wondered why all the profits of their military victories ended up in the hands of the patrician rulers. So in 494 BCE, the plebs gathered outside of the city where one of the army cooks suggested going on strike. They all agreed that was a good idea and shouted, "What's a strike?"

The strike worked, and the plebeians were rewarded with an assembly of their own—the Council of the Plebs. This was not quite a democracy, but it gave everyone a voice in government. Roman citizens could raise concerns and problems and then discuss actions and laws to address those issues. This Roman Republic continued to expand over the next 500 years. It came to include most of Europe and all the lands surrounding the Mediterranean Sea. The republic was headed by two consuls so that no single person would have complete control. There were also senators, who were appointed for life, and various assemblies and magistrates. However, the Roman-controlled territory was so large that it became difficult to manage by the senators and assemblies. In 27 BCE, the Senate recognized Caesar Augustus (adopted nephew of Julius Caesar) as the leader of all Rome. This ended the republic, and the Roman Empire was born.

In 285 CE, Emperor Diocletian divided the Roman Empire into an eastern empire and a western empire. Greek became the language of the eastern Roman Empire. The western empire lasted until in 476 CE when Rome no longer had an emperor. This was followed in Europe by 500 years called the Dark Ages. This was a period of return to the world as it existed before unification under Rome. The eastern Roman Empire continued for another 1,000 years until 1453. By then, the Roman Republic and Roman Empire had existed for 2,000 years. That's a record that may never be broken. The Shang dynasty of 554 years was the longest in Chinese history.

Our modern world has inherited many of the ideas and policies from the early Romans, such as our calendar, languages, our alphabet, and our legal system. But the most significant thing we have from that period 2,000 years ago is democracy with its belief in government by the citizens instead of by an all-powerful dictator or monarch. Citizen involvement in government automatically implied more freedom and fair treatment. These liberal-governing structures were the models for new governments 2,000 years later.

Magna Carta Libertatum

The *Magna Carta Libertatum*, or simply Magna Carta, is recognized as a unique historical compromise between the English monarchy and rebellious barons. It established a council of advisors called parliament and identified some individual liberties. Parliament was not a governing body. It was limited to an advisory role representing the concerns of the upper-middle class. Penned in 1215 CE, the Magna Carta went through occasional renewals, repeals, and rebellions. In 1649, parliament led by Cromwell had enough of the king's interference and decided the country needed a new head. So Charles I was beheaded, and parliament appointed Charles II as the new king. By that time, parliament had assumed most of the power of running the government. In time, the king relinquished even the use of a veto, although technically, he could still use it today. The period from 1215 to 1700 saw a gradual evolution of parliament from a group of advisors to the governing body of citizens. However, this was not without rebellions, conflicts, and several dissolutions and restorations of parliament.

This was a reversal of the process experienced by the Roman Republic. The Roman Republic evolved into having an emperor with an advisory senate, while the English monarchy evolved into having powerful parliament with a symbolic king.

The Greek and Roman republics and the English parliament showed the world that a liberal government run by the citizens was possible and preferable. They provided the inspiration for future generations to fight for self-determination and for freedom from a authoritarian ruler. One big problem that prevented the spread of the liberal democratic form of government was the lack of fast, widespread communications. But as soon as that problem was solved, control of government by the common people quickly replaced many of the traditional monarchies and dictators.

Four Quantum Leaps

For roughly 5,000 years, the concept of democracy was as unimaginable as Netflix. How did the world go from millennia of authoritarian monarchies to the ubiquitous, self-rule, liberal democracies of today? Something happened that changed the course of humanity and governments worldwide.

Today we take for granted smartphones, heart surgeries, global Olympic broadcasts, and democracies. But all these things are recent inventions. The items critical to the development of modern governments did not happen overnight. It evolved slowly after critical breakthroughs.

There were four pivotal points that have drastically transformed civilization. At each of these points, human life changed dramatically. These developments all led to improvements in communications among the populace. Without the progress in communications, it is likely that we would still live in caves, chasing goats and slow-running females.

As the development of communications spread out, so did the demand for liberties, justice, and social cooperation. Liberalism spread around the world a few years behind the wave of advancements in communications.

Language

The first big shift occurred with the development of language. Language developed not long after modern humans evolved the ability to make complex sounds. *Homo sapiens* evolved with a special gene designated the FOXP2 gene. This gene is critical to the ability to pronounce a large variety of sounds. FOXP2 was discovered in 1981 when an English family that could not pronounce words surfaced. After some study, researchers found that members of this family did not have the requisite FOXP2 gene. This was a case of a backward step in evolutionary mutations. Mutations are not always an improvement toward more complex, capable life. In fact, only a tiny percentage of mutations are beneficial, but they lead to survival and reproduction while negative mutations do not survive.

Language has been essential to human progress because it allowed the passing of information from one generation to the next. Each generation did not have to learn critical survival skills on their own. Lessons in everything from childbirth precautions to baking bagels could easily be shared and improved. Language expedited the expansion of agriculture and the migration of *Homo sapiens* around the world. It enabled large populations to work together for the common good. Survival and prosperity has always been better for large groups that could communicate effectively and work together.

Writing

The second quantum leap in human progress was the invention of writing. Numeric symbols evolved before language symbols out of the basic necessity of tracking quantities and transactions.

Perhaps the biggest mistake the Romans made was choosing the useless roman numerals for their numeric system. But they weren't alone because other contemporary numeric systems also used alphabetical characters in nondecimal combinations. The fact that ancient Rome could accomplish so much despite such a serious mathematical handicap Is amazing. Romans are credited with many innovations and accomplishments, such as architecture, legal system, centuries of peace (Pax Romana), universal language (Latin), legal rights of women, networks of paved roads, the dome, and the spread of western culture and Christianity, but they were unable to make any advances in mathematics.

The decimal system and numeric characters we use today are from the arabic system that had evolved with some help from China and India. In 1202, an Italian mathematician Leonardo Fibonacci introduced the arabic numeral system to Europe in his book *Liber Abaci*. This arabic decimal system was behind all scientific progress of the past 500 years. Without a smartphone's calculator app, it would be nearly impossible to solve a simple quadratic equation using roman numerals. Another reason they could not solve simple equations was that they had no idea of what an equation was. Equations and the associated algebra had not been invented yet.

$$Z = VI^{II} + CL\sqrt{XL - IV}$$
$$Z = CMXXXVI$$

We automatically convert roman numerals to our numeric system and then solve the equation. But the decimal characters had not yet been invented. In fact, the Romans did not even have a character for zero.

As clumsy and confusing as roman numerals are, we still have a few stubborn anarchists who, centuries after the Roman Empire collapsed, insist on using them to identify the biggest sporting event in the USA—the Super Bowl. This is so confusing that nobody can remember which Super Bowl their team played in.

Without the invention of writing, we would have no records of the past, no Rosetta Stone in the British Museum, and no White House tweets. Writing evolved around 3000 BCE. Initially, writing systems were collections of pictographs. This gradually changed (except in Japan where they still prefer picture-based writing and manga comics) to having symbols representing sounds instead of nouns. While language helped spread information across generations, writing allowed the spread of information across nations and centuries. Cultures that did not have writing could never advance beyond a Stone Age existence. The evolution of language and the development of writing enabled the emergence of civilization along with its armies and governments. However, for centuries, information was limited to a small percentage of the population who had access to education and to the expensive, manually recorded information.

The Information Revolutions

The next two quantum leaps in communications were the invention of printing and the invention of radio frequency transmissions.

Printing

In Mainz, Germany, Johannes Gutenberg invented fast, flexible printing in 1440. The *Gutenberg Bible* was printed in 1455 and was the first book affordable by people outside of the wealthy class. By 1500, printing presses were in operation all over Europe. The number of printed books exploded into the millions.

This inexpensive and abundant availability of information and ideas resulted in an explosion of literacy among the lower classes. This did not happen overnight. It took decades for the new skill of reading to become a ubiquitous skill. The explosion of printing was the magic key that opened the door to the liberal wave of new ideas and more open-minded attitudes. For the first time in human history, large numbers of people were exposed to information about science, religion, government, economics, and history.

None of the liberal progress of the past 500 years would have been possible without the spread of printing and literacy to the entire population.

The first big liberal revolution that was propagated by the printed word was the Protestant Reformation. This revolution was started by Martin Luther, OSA (Order of Saint Augustine), in 1517. Luther's revolutionary ideas quickly spread throughout Germany and then to the rest of Europe using printed pamphlets. Luther originally proposed changes to the Catholic Church and did not imagine the creation of other Christian churches. The pope saw Luther as just an annoying nuisance and ignored him and his spreading movement until it was too late. Pope Leo X excommunicated Luther, and Luther excommunicated the pope.

With this enormous explosion in information, the ruling classes could no longer control the masses with self-serving censorship of events and general knowledge. This is why dictators routinely destroyed all books and information and even execute educated people as soon as they gain power. Education of the masses is the bane of authoritarian governments. The USA has laws prohibiting the monopolization of media. However, there are conservatives trying to circumvent or repeal these laws. If a group got control of all media channels, they could convince the nation of anything they want, such as invading a neighboring country.

Printing allowed the rapid spread of information and knowledge to everyone. Printing was the breakthrough that got people to question traditional paradigms worldwide. This information revolution led to the Age of Enlightenment (1700s). People questioned everything from science and religion to economics and government. New liberal questions were raised such as government free of religious control, equality of rights for all humans, and a more open-minded approach to everything from sexuality to unorthodox beliefs. The Age of Enlightenment saw the rise of skepticism, reason, and individualism. Liberal philosophies, policies, and practices were characteristics of the Age of Enlightenment.

Printing and reading fostered an accepting attitude to virtually every aspect of life, particularly in politics, sex, and religion. Questions and ideas were raised that previously would never have been considered.

In 1830, Joseph Smith started the Mormon Church in New York State. Also in New York State, a commune, the Oneida Community was started in 1848. The Mormons practiced polygamy. The Oneida Community was more radical and practiced "free love," mating among all 300 members of the community. Nobody was allowed to have exclusive monogamous relations. Only consensual mating was allowed. This helped spread the mating among all members rather than concentrating solely among the few members of both sexes who were in high demand. These developments raised the question of whether or not the sexual revolution started in the 1960s or in the 1860s.

This new, literate world was advancing toward the biggest revolution in history—the worldwide conversion of authoritarian conservative monarchies to revolutionary liberal governments focused on the will of the citizens rather than the wealthy class.

In the late 1700s and the early 1800s, dozens of revolutions occurred throughout South America and Europe. The conservative establishments resisted these demands for changes. In the end, it was impossible to stop the tsunami of power migrating from oligarchs to the working class. These revolutions continued into the 1900s.

Conservatives opposed everything and everyone that is new or different. That is why they are called conservatives. However, after a generation or two, conservative-minded people accepted the liberal accomplishments as if they never opposed them (see Table 2: Major Accomplishments of Liberals.)

The spread of information to all citizens gave them knowledge, power, and motivation to demand control of government and their own destinies. This spread of literacy was perhaps the greatest development in human history. It was the springboard that created the liberal democratic forms of government and subsequent liberal accomplishments we enjoy today.

Radio Frequency Transmission

The science of radio waves (30kHz to 300GHz) traveling through air goes back to their discovery by James Clerk Maxwell in 1864. Scientists Heinrich Hertz and Nikola Tesla performed research and expanded the understanding of radio waves. In 1894, Guglielmo Marconi created the first wireless telegraphy system using these Hertzian waves[10]. This was the first time in history that humans could communicate long distances without being physically connected to each other. This changed our world the same way writing and printing changed our world.

In the following 100 years, we had commercial and military radio, television, cell phones, GPS (global positioning system), communication satellites, streaming movies, and live broadcast around the world of Super Bowl games. Presidential debates could be seen as they occurred in all six time zones of the United States.

Millennials have never known a world without hundreds of TV channels and pocket telephones. *Current events* used to refer to "events of the last week." But now, *current events* refer to "events that have happened since you got out of bed this morning."

For the first 150 years of the United States, most voters were limited to reading what politicians said the day before. But now, they see and hear the candidates in real time. This greatly affected how they feel about a candidate. Abraham Lincoln was not considered photogenic and may not have been elected in the television era. Today the manner in which a speech is given could be more powerful than the actual words used. A candidate could be the most qualified, capable, and experienced of all those running for office, but if he stuttered, mumbled, and appeared to be drunk, few voters would rally to him.

The explosion of all forms of communications has brought most working-class citizens into the political process. It has forced politicians to address issues that directly affect most people. This has been a major factor in expanding the liberal policies of individual rights and freedoms.

PART THREE

The First Law of Politics

In the modern world the stupid are cocksure while the intelligent are full of doubt.

—Bertrand Russell

Ever since the invention of printing in 1440 and the spread of literacy, mankind has been on a gradual migration toward a more liberal world with the expansion of individual freedoms and the acceptance of the equality of all humans regardless of race, religion, or ethnicity. Social conservatives have opposed all forms of social progress

This is the first law of politics: Social Conservatives are always on the wrong side of history.

Independence

Although the social conservatives initially opposed the American Revolution, in time, conservative-minded people realized they were wrong and have accepted the liberal accomplishment of creating a new form of government with ultimate power in the citizens rather than in a monarch. Now many conservatives are so enthusiastic about this liberal accomplishment that they think it was a conservative movement.

Conservatives dislike change. Conservatives fought alongside the British against the liberal colonists in the Revolutionary War to continue their lifestyle as a British colony. Conservatives fought the Civil War against the northern liberals to continue their lifestyle centered on slavery. Liberals prevailed in both wars and gave us the country we have today.

In 1765, the British Parliament realized they were spread very thin financially and needed funds to support their widespread ventures. They got the idea that their American colonies should pay for the war in Canada with France. But they were stuck on exactly how they could get Americans to pay for this war. Parliament argued that the war protected America from invasion by the French Canadians. French Canadians had no plans to invade New York. But parliament needed the money and was persistent. They came up with the unusual idea of taxing all the written words and documents in the colonies. They gave this tax the curious name of the Stamp Act. While they were at it, they threw in a few more unnatural acts like the Sugar Act and Tea Act. The Americans reacted by organizing demonstrations and waving big placards like "Axe the Tax."

At a demonstration in Boston, British soldiers who were frightened by the noisy crowd shot and killed five Americans. They were in America to help and protect the British governor of Massachusetts Bay, Thomas Hutchinson. This event was named the Boston Massacre.

Crispus Attucks was the first one shot. Crispus was a black African American. None of the British soldiers were killed or injured.

John Adams (the second US president) defended the British soldiers in court and was able to get them all acquitted except Matthew Kilroy and Hugh Montgomery. These two faced the death penalty. However, there was a custom called Benefit of Clergy, which excluded clergymen from secular courts. To qualify for this benefit, the accused were required to read Psalm 51:1 of the Bible. To prevent them from ever being able to use the Benefit of Clergy again, the letter *M* was branded on their right thumbs. So the penalty for shooting five Americans was a severe scolding and a warning—"Don't shoot anymore Americans, or you will be in serious trouble"[11].

Confrontations with the British continued. In 1773, Americans made the British Parliament furious by dumping 342 cases of tea into the Boston Harbor rather than pay the tax required by the Tea Act. There then followed a ratcheting up of tension between the Americans and the British in response to each other's actions. Britain sent over many more troops, which eventually led to an actual shooting war that started in 1775 at Lexington, Massachusetts. Nobody knows who fired the first shot.

This is the point at which Americans became divided between conservatives and liberals. Until then, it did not matter much whether you were conservative or liberal because no big decisions or laws were at stake. But as the Revolutionary War started to spread, Americans had to decide which side they would support and which side they would join in battle.

The trademark feature of conservative thinking is the rejection of changes and anything new or different. This attitude can foster stability and survival, but it can also be detrimental when changes and progress are required to adapt to new problems and situations. History has shown that, in the long run, adapting changes slowly and in moderation has yielded the most successful results. Embracing new conventions, technology, and government is not easy and requires intellectual agility and courage.

About 16% of the American colonists feared severe reprisals by the British after the fighting, so they joined the British in fighting against their neighbors. This percentage of conservative Americans has remained roughly the same ever since then. Those fighting alongside the British were called loyalists because they were loyal to King George III. The revolutionary Americans called themselves patriots. The conservative loyalists helped the British by providing them with military intelligence as well as food and lodging to thousands of British troops.

This ideological division between Americans led to very difficult living conditions. A mother would tell her kids to not play with the Miller boys next door because the Millers were the enemy loyalists who wanted to shoot their daddy. After the war, conservatives were deprived of their property. They were exiled to Canada, Great Britain, and the Caribbean Islands.

Benjamin Franklin was one of the most outspoken liberals of the revolutionary period. A public political split came between Franklin and his only son, William Franklin. Benjamin had close ties with London and the British before the war. He managed to have William appointed as the royal governor of New Jersey. Benny and Billy were close and considered each other to be their best friend. When the war started, William considered himself more British than American, so he became a loyalist fighting against the patriots and his father. Despite their deep love for each other, father and son became intractable political enemies as so often happens even today between close family members over political differences. Benjamin disowned his illegitimate son, William, and excluded him from his will.

Washington's Continental Army had an almost impossible task of defeating the world's most powerful army. However, the colonies were fortunate that, at the time, Britain was engaged in the Anglo-French War of 1778–1783 and was forced to allocate most resources to the more serious threat of France. Britain was forced to supplement their troops in the colonies with 30,000 German mercenaries and 19,000 American loyalists.

Early in the war, Washington won very few battles. The Americans tried to get help from France. Initially, France was reluctant to get involved because they did not want to back a loser. However, the stunning defeat of the British in 1777 at Saratoga, New York, was the turning point in the war. General Benedict Arnold's great leadership of the American Army was a major reason for this significant victory. However, he was overlooked and not given any respect or appreciation by the American leaders. This snub greatly upset General Arnold, so he left and joined the British Army where he was given the respect he felt he deserved. It was ironic that Arnold was a key figure in the turning point of the Revolutionary War. Perhaps America would have lost the war, or at least that major battle, without General Arnold.

The Saratoga victory showed that they could defeat the British in America. So France agreed to help the Americans. France provided military supplies and soldiers to join the Continental Army.

The last battle of the war was fought at Yorktown, Virginia. This battle resulted in the unconditional surrender of the British. Washington rejected the surrender condition of amnesty for the American loyalists. The conservative loyalists were considered to be traitors.

There were more French troops at Yorktown than American troops. And the French Navy prevented the British Navy from bringing reinforcements, food, and gunpowder to the British troops at Yorktown. The combined number of soldiers fighting against the British at Yorktown was 18,900. Of this large number of soldiers, only 88 were killed. It is doubtful that America would have won the Revolutionary War without all the French financial, material, and personnel support. Almost 200 years later, the USA returned the favor by helping France defeat the German invaders.

The American liberals fought and died to break away from the traditional form of government prior to the eighteenth century. Conservatives came close to preventing the break from England. Like all progressive accomplishments, it took conservatives some time to realize they had been wrong and to accept the new democratic form of government as an improvement over the British colonial rule.

Slavery

Africans were first captured, put in chains, and taken to the British colonies in America in 1619. 244 years later, slavery was outlawed. However, it was another 100 years before it became illegal to hang citizens for being black. It was common in the South for the local police to organize the hangings themselves. White juries routinely acquitted white men of murdering blacks. Killing your neighbor's cocker spaniel was considered a more serious offense.

After the war, schools and statues were built to honor the defenders of slavery. Nine Southern states—South Carolina, North Carolina,

Georgia, Mississippi, Alabama, Virginia, Tennessee, Texas, and Louisiana—still have legal holidays honoring the leaders who fought to continue their system of slavery[12].

A white jury refused to convict the four white men who set a bomb that killed four young schoolgirls on September 15, 1963. The governor, George Wallace, sent in state troopers to stop the subsequent riots and two young black men were killed. J. Edgar Hoover, head of the FBI, refused to pursue the case. However, 14 years later, the killers were convicted and sentenced to life in prison[13].

Africans were also taken to the Caribbean Islands and to French, Spanish, and Portuguese settlements. These slaves were used primarily on agricultural farms growing sugar, cotton, and turnips. As human nature would have it, slaves were also used for every sort of sexual perversion imaginable and even some unimaginable. Young Southern shoe salesmen and barbers dreamed of the day they could afford to buy an attractive black girl or guy to be his very own sex slave.

In the 1700s, the literate population was still small but growing. Political issues were limited to local and immediate events. By the 1800s, public schools had increased the literate public to nearly 100%. Books, newspapers, and pamphlets were read by nearly everyone. People became better informed about national and international events. They became more familiar with the realities of slavery. The outrage over human bondage spread throughout the industrial northern states and western territories. Liberals were determined to put an end to the horrors of slavery.

The antislavery sentiments had been simmering and growing throughout the country. It reached the boiling point in 1854 when the liberals formed a new political party at a gathering in Ripon, Wisconsin. They named their party the Republican Party. This liberal antislavery party caught on like free money, and nothing could slow its rapid spread across America.

Abraham Lincoln was an antislavery liberal Republican, but he was not well-known around the country. By coincidence, the 1860 Republican convention was held at Chicago in Lincoln's home state of Illinois, where he received enormous support. Lincoln came in a distant second on the first ballot to choose a candidate. After the second and third ballots, Lincoln was close to the nomination but below the minimum required. Then one of the representatives changed his vote, and Lincoln was nominated. America has never been the same since that one vote was cast.

Today Republicans try to take credit for ending slavery because Lincoln was a Republican. However, at the time, this new Republican Party was limited to the North and was very liberal. Southern states were then, and still are, socially conservative. In opposition to the liberal Republicans, Southern conservatives sided with the Democrats. These Southern Democrats became known as Dixiecrats because they believed in strict segregation of African Americans from whites.

Cause of the Civil War

Conservatives always oppose anything or anyone new or different (see definitions of *conservative* and *liberal*.) The Southern conservatives could not imagine how their economy could function if they could not keep all the profits themselves and would have to pay the workers. The Southern slave owners were terrified at the thought of having to pick their own turnips, and they shouted "over my dead body." Well, they didn't mean that literally. What they really meant was "over the dead bodies of all our illiterate, shoeless white farm boys." The poor Southern boys did not own slaves, so defending slavery was not a strong motivation to go get killed. They were told all sorts of lies about how horrible the Yankees were and how the Yanks were coming to take over the Southern states. The farm boys believed these lies and signed up for the Confederate Army. The tactic of lying to the citizens to support a war has been a common practice throughout history.

Today the concept of slavery is so abhorrent that Southern states have taken steps to cover up and rewrite the history of slavery. Southern history books and other sources have ignored the cruelty and inhumanity of slavery as if it never existed. They even have the audacity to claim slaves had it good because they were provided for in a "beneficent and patriarchal system." They have tried to change the cause of the Civil War from slavery to conflicting economics.

It is true that there was a difference in the economies of the North and the South. The North was an urban industrial economy. The South was a rural farming economy. But this was not the prime mover of the secession and Civil War. The inconvenient truth was that the basic cause of the Civil War was slavery. At the time, the Confederate States declared their independence; they felt slavery was natural and nothing to be ashamed of, so they felt no reason to cover up the true reasons for secession or the war. Each state explicitly cited slavery as the cause of secession in their Articles of Secession.

The 1861 Texas Articles of Secession reads as follows:

> These Southern States and their beneficent and patriarchal system of African slavery, proclaiming the debasing doctrine of the equality of all men, irrespective of race or color—a doctrine at war with nature, in opposition to the experience of mankind, and in violation of the plainest revelations of the Divine Law.
>
> By the disloyalty of the Northern States and their citizens and the imbecility of the Federal Government, they demand
> —the abolition of negro slavery throughout the confederacy,
> —the recognition of political equality between the white and the negro races,
> —and avow their determination to press on their crusade against us, so long as a negro slave remains in these States.
>
> For years past this abolition organization has been actively sowing the seeds of discord through the Union, and has rendered the federal congress the arena for

spreading firebrands and hatred between the slave-holding and non-slave-holding States.

The 1861 Georgia Articles of Secession reads as follows:

> The people of Georgia having dissolved their political connection with the Government of the United States of America, present to their confederates and the world the causes, which have led to the separation.
>
> For the last ten years we have had numerous and serious causes of complaint against our non-slave-holding confederate States with reference to the subject of African slavery.
>
> The party of Lincoln, called the Republican Party, under its present name and organization, is of recent origin. It is admitted to be an antislavery party.
>
> While the subordination and the political and social inequality of the African race was fully conceded by all . . .
>
> The feeling of antislavery, which it was well known was very general among the people of the North, had been long dormant or passive; it needed only a question to arouse it into aggressive activity.

Some in the South have tried to change history by denying that the Union won the war but instead claim that both sides just decided to a cease-fire. There was no cease-fire. The Civil War ended in an unconditional surrender by General Robert E. Lee. The South could no longer carry on. They had no ammunition, no food, no supplies; and all sources and transportation of provisions had been destroyed.

The Civil War was, by any measure, the most deadly of all American wars. About 2% of the population was killed in the Civil War, while in each of the many US wars over the years, less than 0.01% of the population was killed. The total killed in the Civil War was more than that in World War I, World War II, and Vietnam War combined. Surgical scrubbing was not practiced until ten years after the war, and antibiotics were not in use until 1930. So many Civil War soldiers died not from bullets but from infections. Also many deaths could have been prevented with helmets, but they were not used until World War I.

The Civil War ended slavery, but it did not end widespread racism in the South. It took several generations and over 150 years to confine racism to only the extreme social conservatives. The institution of slavery would have eventually been terminated without the horrific Civil War. But it is very possible that slavery would have continued for many more decades.

The Thirteenth Amendment to the Constitution, outlawing slavery, was passed in 1865. The liberal Northern states assumed that was the end of slavery and racial issues. They did not anticipate the plethora of racial segregation and persecution laws. These laws were referred to as the Jim Crow laws.

It became obvious that racial equality had to be explicitly spelled out in the Constitution. The Fourteenth Amendment passed in 1868 guaranteed equal treatment of all citizens regardless of race. The Fifteenth Amendment of 1870 outlawed racist policies and laws designed to reduce or prohibit African American citizens from voting.

The Southern conservatives could not accept blacks being treated equally and actually voting, so they came up with indirect and subtle ways of segregation and restricting blacks from voting. A more specific law was required to outlaw extreme racial discrimination.

President John F. Kennedy proposed the extensive Civil Rights Act in 1963 to ensure complete and equal freedom to all Americans in every area of society. The Southern states were determined to block this law. They conducted a 75-day filibuster. A former Ku Klux Klan member, conservative Senator Byrd of West Virginia, spoke for 15 hours. However, they failed to kill the bill, and it was passed on July 2, 1964.

However, Southern conservatives still managed to suppress black voting through reduced voting centers, gerrymandering, and unjustified purges of voter registrations. To address this suppression of voting, the Voting Rights Act was passed in 1965. This was a big help in allowing all citizens to vote. However, in 2018, the conservative Supreme Court decided that voter suppression was not illegal. So the next day, several conservative states passed minority-voter suppression laws.

Although democracy is an important, valuable right of Americans, conservatives have constantly come up with ways to suppress voting and to curtail true democracy. Conservatives knew that if the US had a true democracy where everyone voted, winning elections would be more difficult for them.

In 1963, Mississippi State was in the NCAA college championship tournament and Loyola, an integrated team, was next on their schedule. But Mississippi schools were barred from playing against teams that had any black players. The Mississippi team had to travel in secret to the game so they could play without alerting anyone. There also was a rule that only a limited number of black players could be on the court at the same time. Loyola won the game by ten points and won the national championship. Two years later, Mississippi State had black players on the team[14].

As recently as 1970, Americans of African heritage were still prohibited from playing on the University of Alabama's football team. That year, the all-white Alabama team played against the University of Southern California team. The USC backfield was comprised of all black players including the quarterback. Both teams had national championship aspirations. USC ran all over the Alabama team with its slower, smaller, all-white players. Alabama was embarrassed 42–21. The Alabama alumnus and alumna demanded that the coach, Bear Bryant, either get the best players regardless of race or get a new job.

And so ended the last formal hold out to segregation in sports—a full century after the Civil War ended. But racism itself continued.

Southern social conservatives opposed the abolition of slavery for many decades, but eventually, conservative-minded people realized they had been wrong and have accepted the liberal accomplishment of ending slavery. In fact, Southerners have so fully embraced the abolition of slavery that some are now trying to take credit for ending slavery.

History has proven that social conservatives were wrong to oppose the abolition of slavery and the segregation of blacks. (See the "First Law of Politics"—social conservatives are always on the wrong side of history.)

Women Voting

Social conservatives initially opposed allowing women to vote, but in time, conservatives got used to the idea and realized they had been wrong. Within only a few elections, conservatives accepted this liberal accomplishment allowing women to vote.

Before 1900, very few countries allowed women to vote. By 2000, women in all progressive countries were allowed to vote. This is another example of the migration of civilization from the outdated, conservative world of autocratic kings, serfs, and sequestered women to the liberal world of democratically elected leaders.

The original constitution allowed only 2% of the population to vote. But it became increasingly difficult to defend this limited constituency as liberal policies and philosophies continued to spread throughout the civilized world. The Continental Congress of 1785 believed that the uneducated, illiterate lower classes did not understand all the complexities of economics and foreign relations, so voting was limited to males who were property owners. Also Catholics, Jews, and Quakers were barred from voting probably because it was thought they would demand Christian prayers in schools and other peculiar religious concessions such as tax exemptions for religious organizations.

Alexander Hamilton was outspoken on allowing only upper-class men to vote:

> All communities divide themselves into the few and the many. The first are the rich and the well-born; the other the mass of the people . . . turbulent and changing, they seldom judge or determine right. Give therefore to the

wealthy first class a distinct, permanent share in the Government . . . Nothing but a permanent body can check the imprudence of democracy.

Early in the 1800s, giving women the freedom to vote kept popping up but gained no real traction. Women's suffrage became an issue in 1848 at a convention in Seneca Falls, New York. Susan Anthony and Elizabeth Stanton were the leaders of the movement to allow women to vote.

After African Americans were given the right to vote with the Fifteenth Amendment in 1870, people started to ask "Hey, what about women?" But in the 1800s, social conservatives considered women intellectually inferior and excessively emotional.

Some antisuffragist quotes[15] are as follows:

—"Women would be corrupted by politics and chivalry would die out."
—"They would stop marrying, having children, and the human race would die out."
—"Women are emotional creatures and incapable of making a sound political decision."
—"The vast majority of women have no desire for the vote."
—"Women have at present a vast indirect influence through their menfolk on the politics of this country."

It became a long 70-year struggle for women's rights. In 1920, a constitutional amendment required a minimum of 36 states to agree to ratify it. 35 states had approved the measure when Tennessee brought it up for a vote. All the other remaining states had rejected the amendment. The Tennessee vote to ratify was passed by a count of 50–49. The Nineteenth Amendment to the Constitution allowing women to vote was finally passed by a single vote.

Although both Republicans and Democrats voted to allow women to vote, the vote was split between conservatives and liberals. Conservatives voted against letting nonwhites and ex-slaves vote—the Fifteenth Amendment. Conservatives also voted against letting women vote—the Nineteenth Amendment. In 1920, Southern voters, regardless of party, were strongly conservative as most still are today. They were the biggest voting block that opposed women voting.

As with all liberal progress, over time conservatives realized they had been wrong in opposing the right of women to vote. Eventually, conservatives caught up with liberals, and today, they fully accept women voting.

Worker's Rights

Social liberals have always had to fight for worker's rights and decent treatment by employers. Today we take for granted the good working conditions and benefits that workers have, but it was not always like this. Before worker unions and labor laws, factory employees suffered horrible working conditions[16]. In textile mills of 1912, workers were killed in industrial accidents, five-year-old children were employed, and 60-hour workweeks at subsistence wages were the norm. Paid vacations, health insurance, pensions, and disability benefits were unheard of. Living conditions were also terrible. Families shared small factory-owned shacks and beds. Diseases spread because of unsanitary living conditions. Factory owners made millions while the life expectancy for mill workers was 32 years or about half of that for the general population.

In Lawrence, Massachusetts, 25,000 mill workers went on strike. The city police and the state militia suppressed and attacked the workers who were on strike. One worker Annie LoPizzo was shot and killed by the police. This murder of a worker led to the support of people all across America. Eventually the employers relented, and workers were given raises, overtime pay, and safer working conditions.

Many workers were murdered in other strikes[17]. Police shot Anthony Giuseppe in a 1902 coal-mine strike. Police beat Joseph Beddall to death during a strike demonstration that same year. William Durham was shot and killed during a strike in Brownsville, Pennsylvania. These are just a few of the many striker killings.

The plight of the suffering workers drew national attention, just as the realities of slavery had done 60 years earlier. Social liberals demanded changes to the exploitation of American workers by the conservative, superwealthy class. However, the three conservative presidents of the 1920s had no interest in reforms to help workers. It was not until the liberal-minded Franklin Delano Roosevelt was elected in 1932 that labor abuses were addressed[18].

The National Labor Relations Act of 1935 legitimized labor unions and required employers to negotiate working conditions, wages, and hours. This was a significant change from the old paradigm that had existed since the beginning of the Industrial Revolution where workers' complaints were routinely ignored. The passage of this bill generated a dramatic surge in union membership.

In 1938, the liberal Congress under Roosevelt passed the Fair Labor Standards Act. This act outlawed child labor, established a minimum wage, set the eight-hour workday, and overtime. The Social Security Act was passed in 1935. It provided for worker pensions, unemployment insurance, and aid to dependent children. These liberal policies changed the worker-employer relationship. Workers received respect and were treated with dignity. Their health and well-being could no longer be ignored. Years later, these liberal accomplishments would be taken for granted by everyone including conservatives.

Before these liberal changes improved the living conditions of the working class, factory workers were at the bottom of the income ladder. But by the 1950s, a large middle class emerged and workers could buy comfortable homes and cars with air conditioners. Labor unions and labor laws helped create a new middle-class culture where working families could visit national parks on weekends, join Little Leagues, and send their kids to local colleges.

Worker rights is another area where liberals led the way to our modern society with fairness and equality for everybody.

In the future, people will find it incredible that in 2019, conservatives opposed background checks, opposed legalized cannabis, opposed the environmental protections, opposed net neutrality, opposed the Affordable Care Act, opposed gay marriage, and opposed Consumer Financial Protection Bureau (CFPB).

Health Care

Republicans are eager to claim they are the party of social conservatives. Republicans and social conservatives always oppose changes in their world. They have always staunchly opposed all national health-care programs.

Democrat president Harry Truman first proposed universal health care in 1949. The social conservatives joined with the American Medical Association and the pharmaceutical companies to oppose Truman's proposal. Health care was brought up again when Republican Gerald Ford was president. It did not get very far because Ford promised to veto any health-care system. Later, Democrat president Bill Clinton tried to get a health-care bill passed. But again social conservatives and special interests launched a major effort to suppress the proposed health-care bill.

Democrat Barack Obama was elected president in 2008. At the same time, Democrats gained control of the House and Senate and passed the Affordable Care Act (ACA) over the Republican opposition. The ACA, also known as Obamacare, became law in 2010. Republican policy at the time was to automatically oppose everything Democrats proposed regardless of what the voters wanted or needed. The ACA was criticized as disastrous socialism with the government controlling every aspect of health care. Republicans also made up the lie that health care would be rationed out and government panels, dubbed Death Panels, would have to decide who received care and lived or who did not and died.

Contrary to the Republican claims, the ACA is not a government-run socialist takeover of the health-care industry. The ACA is an insurance-access program and not a national health-care system as most other countries have. Also the ACA did not include those imaginary death panels. These false attacks became a rallying cry for social conservatives in elections for the next seven years.

Republicans twice challenged the legality of Obamacare in the Supreme Court and lost each time. Republicans were confident that the Supreme Court would rule against the ACA. Although five of the nine justices were Republican appointees, Republicans lost the first challenge in 2012 by a vote of 5–4. Republicans lost the second challenge in 2015 by a vote of 6–3. It became clear that the social conservatives' scare tactics were nothing but false political propaganda. Republicans did not like the Affordable Care Act because it is recognized as another liberal accomplishment and Republicans put party concerns above what is good for Americans.

When Republicans gained control of all three branches of government in 2016, they faced a dilemma they could not solve. On one hand, they were opposed, as they always have been, to any government involvement in health care, while on the other hand, there was a strong public demand to keep the ACA.

Social conservatives were forced into proposing a health-care program of some kind. They would never propose any health-care program if they were not forced into it by popular demand. After decades of steadfast opposition, social conservatives now realize voters would no longer tolerate politicians working for the highly profitable corporate health-care industry instead of for their constituencies.

Realizing they would have trouble winning elections, Republicans finally gave in and proposed an alternative to the ACA. They tried several times to propose a health-care program that met their competing goals of continuing high-profit margins built into the corporate monopolies of health care while also meeting the demands of Americans for affordable health-care insurance. High profits and high levels of service are incompatible goals.

The conservative plan for health insurance did not address major issues that people wanted in health care. The proposed alternative to the ACA did not include coverage of preexisting conditions because they cut into the profits of the health-care industry. And that was unacceptable to Republicans.

There is no disagreement that the ACA needs adjustments; however, the basic concept of a government-assisted insurance program is now endorsed by 55% of the voters[19]. All other developed countries have had some form of universal health care for the past 50 years. Health care in these other countries is assumed to be one of the basic human needs along with safety and security.

Health care is another area where social conservatives have opposed the liberal progress that the rest of the world has embraced.

Prostitution

Prostitution is legal in many countries and in Nevada. As long as it involves consenting adults, there are no victims. There is no reason natural relations between adults should be illegal. Yet conservatives insist on continuing these outdated and ineffective laws criminalizing a person's right to earn a living even though no one is harmed in the process. Texas conservatives proposed a law outlawing prostitution involving robots[20]. Maybe Texans want to protect the robots from abuse and exploitation.

Unlike violent crimes, opinions on prostitution are far from unanimous. Slightly more people think we should legalize prostitution. 49% favor legalization, while 44% do not[21]. The reasons for not legalizing it are not consistent or persuasive. Like so many other issues, it is just a matter of personal feelings and opinions.

Our sex laws are leftovers from the prudish period of the 1800s, before swimming suits were invented. Forcing prostitution underground contributes to the spread of sexually transmitted diseases. Under legalized prostitution, sex workers in the USA would be tested for diseases before getting permits. Physical exams are standard requirements in countries with legalized prostitution. Instead, prostitutes usually work in unhealthy environments, are put in jail, and are labeled as criminals. Today, clients can contract diseases and spread the diseases to other innocent people before they realize they are a carrier. People have died after sex with a partner who did not even know they were carriers of an infectious, fatal disease.

Millions of women, especially struggling students, feel that getting paid for engaging in sexual activities is an easy way to pay the rent. But they do not want to be arrested for prostitution, so they try to find a sugar daddy. One sugar-daddy site has about a million members, and 35% are students[22]. There are about ten women online looking for a sugar daddy for every sugar daddy looking for a sugar baby. This big difference means it is a sugar-daddy market. Therefore, it is not as lucrative for the ladies as they have been led to believe.

It is hard to make a case against legalizing prostitution when, in one form or another, it is accepted and practiced by virtually everyone, including good girls and boys from good families.

Libertarians and liberals believe people should be allowed to make a living any way they choose as long as nobody is harmed. It is a question of freedom.

If conservatives were consistent, they would insist that pornography actors and actresses be arrested for getting paid to perform sex acts. This is exactly what prostitution is, yet one is legal and the other is not. They justify this by claiming the porno prostitute is paid by a third party, so that makes it OK. The morality aspect is never an issue. Our sex laws serve no rational purpose.

It is not clear why prostitution is illegal. It seems everyone has a different explanation. In any case, the laws are about as effective as our drug laws, which have done nothing to eliminate illegal drug trafficking. The main obstacle to legalizing prostitution is the widespread prudish attitude that is more prevalent in the US than in other countries except Muslim countries. Americans have hypocritical attitudes regarding sex.

Like drugs, a lot of public money is wasted on law enforcement and on incarceration of people convicted of nothing more serious than private, personal behavior that does not harm anyone. Instead of wasting many millions on enforcing archaic sex laws, the government could receive tax revenues from sensibly regulated sex businesses.

Prostitution is another issue where social conservatives oppose social progress.

Prudes and Nudes

Conservative thinking has kept sex repressed in the United States as if it were some shocking immorality. Many conservative-minded people consider all sexuality to be immoral with the only exception being between married couples of opposite sex.

Other countries, like Spain for example, have no laws prohibiting nudity. Nude beaches and resorts are perfectly legal in many countries. There are private nudist facilities in the US, but all public nudity is illegal. It is not clear what harm is caused when a topless matron is seen on a beach, but it is against the law. All cities have strict laws prohibiting topless and nude entertainment even though there is no purposeful justification for these laws. Entertainment and media have lists of rules controlling language, visuals, and sexual content of any kind. Humorist George Carlin in a monologue ridiculed seven words that are forbidden to be uttered on TV[23].

Anything regarding sex is a more sensitive subject in conservative America than in most modern cultures. Even common, everyday language feels the impact of sexually repressed, conservative thinking. In the past, we were so embarrassed about everything sexual that we invented phrases to avoid speaking plainly as mature adults. Instead of using adult English words, we use ambiguous phrases like *sleeping with*, *making love*, *having sex*, and *private parts*. We do this to avoid using proper but supposedly embarrassing words. It seems people have the attitude that if we avoid using the correct words, the embarrassing subject does not exist.

We are not so intellectually immature; we must avoid using legitimate adult words such as *mating*, *fellatio*, *fornicating*, *copulating*, *penis*, *vagina*, or even *screwing* and *fucking*. But we are still subjected to reading these puritanical anachronistic phrases even in newspapers and sophisticated, serious publications. It is time to grow up and use real words instead of coded, childish phrases.

Marriage counselors recognize that there are elements of sexual incompatibility in nearly every divorce. Yet people are too embarrassed to even mention the subject of sexual compatibility prior to the wedding. Many even believe there should be no premarital sex at all, which guarantees there will be divorces because of sexual incompatibility. One example is the couple that got divorced immediately after the honeymoon because the bride was shocked to learn the meaning of the word *fellatio*.

Instead of accepting sex as normal human behavior, conservative Americans are too embarrassed to even talk about things like legalizing prostitution and spousal sexual compatibility. So instead of accepting and dealing with our human nature, we endure all the pain and suffering of divorces and dangerous street prostitution.

Sex laws and attitudes are also areas where conservatives have been on the wrong side of history.

Illegal Drugs

All the issues regarding legalized sex apply to legalized drugs and to gambling. Conservatives have always fought against every effort to legalize the use of cannabis or marijuana. In 1936, a church group backed a movie titled *Reefer Madness*. This movie depicted marijuana users involved in hallucinations, suicide, manslaughter, rape, and descent into madness. Today the movie is considered to be an amusing satire on drug use. The movie is a great example of how conservatives manipulate public opinion with disinformation. Movie critics have panned it as one of the worst films ever made. But conservatives believe the movie is an accurate portrayal of what happens to those who smoke marijuana.

Liberals are more open-minded to social changes than conservatives (see "Dictionary Definitions") and realize that cannabis does not affect people the way conservatives think it does. About 64% of Americans now approve of legalizing marijuana. 29 states have passed laws allowing the use of cannabis for medical reasons, and nine states now allow cannabis for recreational use. In 2018, Canada approved cannabis for recreational use. It is time for the conservative politicians to accept the use of marijuana and pass federal laws legalizing it.

War on Drugs

Studies have been conducted to define the positive and negative effects of alcohol and marijuana. It is not clear whether cannabis or alcohol is the more dangerous drug. Neither one should be consumed before driving. There are legitimate medical uses of cannabis but not for alcohol. And alcohol use is related to several medical problems. At the federal level, alcohol is legal, while cannabis is not legal. Eventually, the federal laws will become obsolete. But until they are repealed, there will remain banking laws that prohibit using banks for money obtained in criminal activities. This has been a problem for the expansion of legal marijuana businesses.

Other drugs can be more addictive and problematic. However, there is disagreement on how to minimize the impact of these drugs on individuals and society.

The war on drugs was started officially by President Nixon in 1971. However, that was just an extension of the law enforcement that had been in effect for 50 years. This war has not yet enjoyed victory or even any significant progress in reducing drug use. The only significant accomplishment of the war on drugs is the same as that for prostitution—the employment of millions of law enforcement and judicial personnel. It is also a bottomless pit for your taxes.

In the past two decades, there has been no change in the use of hard drugs like cocaine[24]. The use of cannabis and opioids has been steadily increasing for years[25]. The war on drugs has created underground markets and murderous gangs in the USA, Mexico, and Central America.

An alternative to the war on drugs is the decriminalization of personal use of drugs. In 2001, Portugal became the first country to decriminalize drugs including marijuana, cocaine, heroin, and methamphetamine. Several other countries—including Spain, Italy, and Mexico—have since also decriminalized personal use of drugs. But did it work? The number of drug users in Portugal has declined from 100,000 to 25,000 (26).

> "Judging by every metric, decriminalization in Portugal has been a resounding success," says Glenn Greenwald, an attorney, author and fluent Portuguese speaker, who conducted the research. "It has enabled the Portuguese government to manage and control the drug problem far better than virtually every other Western country does."
>
> The *Cato* paper reports that between 2001 and 2006 in Portugal, rates of lifetime use of any illegal drug among seventh through ninth graders fell from 14.1% to 10.6%; drug use in older teens also declined. Lifetime heroin use among 16-to-18-year-olds fell from 2.5% to 1.8% (although there was a slight increase in marijuana use in that age group). New HIV infections in drug users fell by 17% between 1999 and 2003, and deaths related to heroin and similar drugs were cut by more than half. In addition, the number of people on methadone and buprenorphine treatments for drug addiction rose to 14,877 from 6,040, after decriminalization, and money saved on enforcement allowed for increased funding of drug-free treatment as well[26].

The Bureau of Justice Statistics reports that about 25% of incarcerations are for drug offenses. If crimes tied to drug use, such as burglary, are included, the percentage is 36%. This means that about one-third of the total amount of money spent on courts, prisons, police, probation, parole, and public defenders is due to illegal drugs.

California has 34 prisons, and the annual cost for each inmate is $70,810. The budget for prisons is about $11 billion[27]. Decriminalizing drugs would save about $2 billion in California. If all states are included and all courts, lawyers, and police are also included, the savings would be in the hundreds of billions of dollars[28].

What happens after decriminalization of drugs?

Danny, a drug user, stops breaking into homes stealing 65-inch HD TVs that he sells for 50 dollars. He also stops hanging out at the local crack house. Instead, he goes to the neighborhood drug clinic where he is treated as a medical patient rather than as a criminal. Eventually, the market for illegal drugs is greatly diminished and even eliminated in many areas.

Without a viable, profitable market, drug dealers are not making much money, so they would get new jobs as chiropractors or as politicians. Without a steady supply of convicted meth users, the number of prison guards and cooks is reduced. These people would also find other lines of employment, such as fashion photographers or as stock-market salesmen. This could lead to a reduction in your state taxes. However, it is more likely that your taxes would remain the same while the unspent state revenue is redirected to lowering university tuitions and to buying the new self-driving police cars.

A secondary effect of the reduced drug market is the lack of incentive for drug gangs in Central America to export drugs to the States. Over time, these drug gangs would have to lay off their employees and their armies and the practice of murdering young men who refused to join the gangs would be unnecessary. Thousands of Guatemalans would no longer become refugees escaping the gang wars in Limonada. The USA would save the $20 billion that is estimated for the border wall. This unspent money would pay for all the new drug clinics.

So in the end, decriminalization of drug use would reduce crimes and gangs, would reduce taxes, would reduce illegal immigration, and would end the failed war on drugs. Unfortunately, conservatives continue to believe the billion-dollar war on drugs is the only way to reduce the number of drug users even though that has never happened.

PART FOUR

American Exceptionalism

I do not know which makes a man more conservative— to know nothing but the present, or nothing but the past.

—John Maynard Keynes

The observation here is that conservative thinking has kept America from accepting the norms and conventions adapted by the rest of the world.

We usually think of conservatives only in the political sense, but conservatives have had a big influence in areas outside of politics. Conservatives have influenced so many areas that the US is now different from virtually all other countries. This uniqueness has been labeled American exceptionalism. This phrase can be interpreted in many ways, but here, the meaning is limited to the differences between America and all other countries.

Many people object to this phrase because it seems to imply that Americans think they are better than everyone else. National pride is normal for everyone, but the idea of superiority raises images of big swastika banners and the Aryan master race. To avoid confusion, the word *exceptional* is used here as defined in the dictionary—"unusual, not typical."

Although there are minor cultural and genetic differences among groups of people, in general, people are essentially the same all over the world. We all want security, opportunity to provide for our families, personal freedoms, and fair treatment. Everyone wants "life, liberty, and the pursuit of happiness." We are tempted to focus on minor differences and see them as markers of people who are completely different from who we are.

The more isolated a group is, the more likely it will, over time, drift in different directions from other groups. This is how *Homo sapiens* have acquired different languages, different physical features, and different cultures and religions even though we all remain a single biological species.

The Atlantic and Pacific Oceans made the United States relatively isolated from the other cultural and economic centers of the world. The US population has been expanding and growing ever since Columbus revealed to Europeans his great secret of how to sail east across the Atlantic back to Europe. Without the knowledge of how to sail east across the Atlantic, any trip west to the new land was a one-way trip. That was unacceptable, and it would have discouraged any settlements until the invention of the airplane. Few people realize that Columbus's knowledge of sailing the Atlantic is what really changed the world. Columbus knew that the secret to sailing east was to follow the North Atlantic Current north and then east. He is never given credit for this great accomplishment.

The large separation from Europe contributed to the sense of independence from European influence. This isolation created differences between the US and other countries. The US has been much more conservative and reluctant to accept the progress made in other countries.

Weights and Measures

The system used for weights and measures in the US is referred to as the imperial system. It evolved over many centuries past. The *mile* goes all the way back to the Roman Empire, where a *mile* was the equivalent of a thousand paces—*mīlle passus* in Latin. The *foot* has also been used since ancient times, but it changed from place to place and from time to time, depending on what size shoe the current king wore.

Other sizing units in the imperial system have disparate origins—never based on any coherent, rational, or even decimal organization. As a result, nobody knows how many teaspoons are in a tablespoon (2.9 tsp.) or how many square feet are in an acre (43,560 sq. ft.) or how many yards are in a mile (1,760 yds.).

Although this ancient system is incomprehensible and confusing, it was decided that this should be the system used in the US. No other country uses this illogical archaic system.

The metric system was developed to solve the problems of the confusing and inconsistent imperial system. The imperial system did not even have scientific standards to officially define the basic units to a high degree of accuracy. The metric system was first used in 1799 during the French Revolution. The definition of a *meter* was set to be one ten millionth of the distance from the equator to the North Pole. It has since been changed to be the distance light travels in 0.00000000333 seconds. So now, if you ever want to measure your living room for a new carpet in meters, all you have to do is measure how many nanoseconds it takes light to travel across the room.

The metric system quickly became accepted around the world because the units are decimal multiples of each other. Conversions no longer required recalling hard-to-remember conversion factors. Conservatives are slow to accept anything new or different, so American conservatives kept the US stuck with the old imperial system of metrics. Below are the measures using the metric system. The last line shows measures using the imperial system.

1 kilometer = 1,000 meters
1 meter = 100 centimeters
1 centimeter = 10 millimeters
1 gram = 1,000 milligrams
1 mile = 5,280 feet = 1,760 yards

Conversion consistency is not the only problem. Do-it-yourself weekend mechanics and handymen are required to have two sets of tools—metric and imperial. When working on their boats and motorcycles, they often do not know which tools to use, so they keep trying different socket wrenches until they find one that fits or else they shout "screw it" and grab an adjustable Channellock plier. This usually destroys the nut and causes bleeding someplace. This aspect of American exceptionalism is seldom recognized.

Embarrassing examples of American exceptionalism in science occurred in September 1999 and again in 2006. NASA's Mars Climate Orbiter (MCO) made it to Mars then disintegrated into its atmosphere. NASA subcontractor Lockheed Martin created thruster software that used imperial units, not the metric units NASA assumed. As a result, the control program did not make the conversion and the orbiter entered Mars's atmosphere at a lower trajectory than it needed and the engines failed because of overheating. The NASA policy of using both metric and imperial units led to the loss of the entire $125 million Mars climate probe mission.

In 2006, a NASA spacecraft was scheduled to dock with a military satellite. But due to a conversion error that was overlooked, the spacecraft crashed into the satellite. The reason NASA was still using two measurement systems was that the management considered it too expensive to convert everything to metric. Now all NASA work is only in metric.

The main reasons the USA did not jettison the archaic imperial system was the strong opposition of conservatives and the costs of changing all the highway signs. Another reason was that uniquely American sports would have some unusual numbers. For example, a football field would be 91.44 meters instead of 100 yards. One social conservative expressed the attitude of many conservatives when she said, "Those other countries should change to our system." It seems inevitable that someday the US will catch up with the rest of the world in metrics.

Temperature

The US is the only country that measures temperature in Fahrenheit degrees. The rest of the world use degrees Celsius. Daniel Fahrenheit, a Dutch physicist, proposed the Fahrenheit scale in 1724. There are various accounts of how he came up with his temperature scale with water freezing and boiling at the odd points of 32°F and 212°F. One of the accounts had something to do with a dartboard.

18 years after Fahrenheit proposed his temperature scale, a Swedish astronomer, Andy Celsius, heard about it and thought it was a joke. So in 1742, Celsius proposed his temperature scale with freezing and boiling at the logical values of 0°C and 100°C, respectively. The entire world agreed that the Celsius scale was preferred. It didn't help that everyone had trouble remembering how to spell ~~Farenhiet~~ *Fahrenheit*. In 1970, the few countries that still had been clinging to Fahrenheit changed to Celsius. So now, 205 out of 206 countries use the Celsius scale while Americans are constantly converting Celsius to Fahrenheit as they travel in foreign countries.

Americans could benefit from remembering that

- 13°C (55°F) is cold
- 23°C (73°F) is nice
- 33°C (91°F) is hot

Time

The US is one of the few countries where the time of day is not expressed in hours from 0 to 24. Instead, Americans prefer to count up to 12 twice and then add *a.m.* or *p.m.* This is not because Americans have trouble remembering what numbers come after 12. European countries plus Russia and Japan use the 24-hour time method.

The 24-hour day has roots in ancient times. Back then, they had no interior lighting other than fire, so it was common to stop counting the hours of the day at sunset. The first public clock that struck the hours was built in Italy. When a bell rings the number of the hour every hour of the day for 24 hours (i.e, 300 times!), a large amount of ropes and gears is required. This complex arrangement was not reliable, so it was suggested that they hire a few unemployed hunchbacks to ring the bells. After a while, the hunchbacks became deaf from all the bell ringing and would often lose count of the rings around 15 or 19. Also, people were annoyed with the incessant ringing all night long when they were trying to sleep. So they fired the hunchbacks and replaced the 24-hour clocks with 12-hour clocks that would go around twice. Everyone was happy and the hunchbacks went off to be lab assistants in spooky hilltop castles.

Although the US is a 12-hour country, organizations that require accuracy and must avoid confusion use the 24-hour method. Hospitals, law enforcement, military, and others could accidently refer to 8:12 when they really mean 20:12, or 8:12 p.m. So they all use the international standard of 24-hour time notation.

Digital watches are much friendlier to the 24-hour method. This explains why young adults and people who travel prefer electronic watches to mechanical watches. One reason everyone does not use electronic watches is that Rolex does not make a $5,000 digital watch. When Cartier sells $3,500 digital wristwatches, mechanical watches will become historical collector items.

These strange, illogical systems of measurements are good examples of American exceptionalism and of intransigent conservatives who always oppose anything new or different no matter how sensible (See table 1: Definitions).

Sports

The US went its own way in team sports as it did in metrics. While games similar to soccer and baseball had been played in England and other countries for centuries, basketball and football are uniquely American sports that arose in the late 1800s.

Soccer

Soccer is the oldest team sport in the world. Soccer has only two main rules. All the other rules are incidental. The two rules are these: don't use your hands and get the ball into the goal.

References have been found describing soccer-type competitions in ancient Rome and in China. It was not unusual for one village to have an imbalance in the number of females and males. So a village chief would suggest a raid on the neighboring village to acquire more blushing young virgins. But the villagers were not stupid and shouted, "Are you crazy? They got knives and spears." So they agreed to a soccer match with the victors getting tickets to the Saturday dance where they could meet pretty maidens looking for husbands. This is why soccer became the most popular team sport in the world. Soccer also became popular because spectators could go home to get some bangers and mash in the middle of the game and not miss any of the action. When they returned an hour later, the score would still be 0–0.

It is not clear why soccer did not become popular in the United States. It is probably because soccer did not give its players the chance to smash into the opposing players. Americans like to smash into things.

Football

Football is not a conservative-liberal issue. However, it is uniquely American in a world where the universal sport is soccer. As such, it deserves a brief discussion here.

The prohibition against handling the ball in soccer was too frustrating for impatient Americans, so they changed the rules to allow handling the ball and even throwing the ball to teammates. And just to be different, Americans outlawed kicking the ball down the field. This made American football exclusive to the US.

The National Football League (NFL) may be the most valuable sports league in the world. Teams are valued at about $3 billon each. The NFL is worth more than the Major League Baseball and the National Basketball Association teams combined. A few of the NFL players are paid over $25 million per year. But this is only half of the $51 million that the best soccer player, Lionel Messi, earned playing for Barcelona. The average salary for both soccer and football players is around $2 million per year.

American football is the most challenging sport in terms of strategic and tactical complexity. It is more complicated than chess because everything is constantly changing and dozens of options have to be evaluated every few seconds. Not only is the situation on the field changing but several other factors must also be taken into account. A major concern is which players are in the game at the time. The best payers may not be in the game for many reasons such as injuries, suspensions, or equipment problems. Other major factors are game time and score. So the most important person on the team may be the coach on the sideline constantly deciding what to do next.

Every team issues a team playbook to their player that describes all the dozens of formations and individual assignments for hundreds of plays. In the past, these playbooks were bigger than a Chicago city phone book and players had to memorize every play for more than one position. Now, every player is given a small computer with playbooks installed. If a player has difficulty memorizing the hundreds of plays, dozens of offensive formations, and the secret-coded language, the coach puts him on the defensive line and tells him "Just find the guy with the ball and throw him on the ground."

Some players have trouble remembering all the plays, so they copy the plays to their smartphones and hide them in their jockstraps to look at during the game. This also affords them the ability to check in with their parole officers at halftime.

In preparing to play a game, players and football team coordinators spend countless hours studying and analyzing everything the opponent does in each of dozens of game situations. At game time, an assistant keys in all the conditions of the current game situation as it occurs and the computer immediately summarizes everything that the opponent has done in similar situations in the past and creates a report that displays a chart of probabilities for each type of play the opponent is likely to run. The team coordinator then selects a corresponding response to counter the opponent. It becomes a game of matching wits with the opponent's coordinator. No other sport comes close to this level of tactical complexity.

Football teams have two players on the offense squad called tackles. These tackles are forbidden to actually tackle anyone. They are not even allowed to wrap their arms around defensive players. If they do, their team is given a big penalty. That's why offensive tackles are always standing around looking confused.

Football is the only sport where all the players are replaced every time possession of the ball changes hands. Immediately after the change of possession, all 22 players run off the field to inhale oxygen on the sideline and 22 different players run onto the field. This happens continuously throughout the game. No other team sport has all the players running on and off the field every few minutes. Originally, football teams could not change players at any time. And most players played the entire game. The rules were changed to allow highly specialized position players to be put in the game depending on the game situation.

It is headline news when an outside linebacker is reassigned to play middle linebacker even though there is little difference in what is required of them. By the way, all middle linebackers are named Mike. This is because coaches can't remember the names of all the players. If a middle linebacker is named Isaiah, they call him Mike anyway.

There is no other sport like football, wherein the players stop playing dozens of times to hold a conference and vote on who gets stuck holding the ball when play resumes. They usually force the guy with the fewest friends on the team hold the ball. That way, they avoid a lot of broken bones and have longer playing careers.

American football is also the only sport where serious injuries like broken bones and concussions are routine occurrences. In fact, there are so many injuries that a team never has the same players in every game. Every game is played with a different set of players. At the end of the season, the top prize, called the Lombardi Trophy, is awarded to the team with the most players able to stand without their agents holding them up and who have not lately smashed their fist into their girlfriend's face.

Someday in the future, football will be as popular around the world as soccer is. Today the NFL draws big sellout crowds for games played in London and in Mexico City. International expansion is always being studied. For those who understand the sport, it is a lot more complicated and interesting than any other sport.

Baseball and Basketball

Games similar to baseball had been played in the 1700s in England and other countries, but they had no official rules or professional teams. Team sports were informal, unorganized affairs played by groups from rival parishes, villages, and factories. In 1845, baseball groups in New York City published the first formal set of rules. These rules added the new force-out rule. The first professional team, the Cincinnati Red Stockings, was formed in 1869. Baseball was referred to as America's game for over 100 years. But by the twenty-first century, professional football surpassed all American spectator sports in popularity.

Basketball is the only sport that did not evolve out of some informal sandlot game. It was created by Dr. Naismith in Springfield, Massachusetts, in 1891. Dr. Naismith was a PE instructor from Canada. He did not have any coaching work during the long winters between football season and baseball season. So to avoid getting fired, he came up with basketball. Basketball got its name from the peach baskets that were the original goals.

Team athletics in the USA are unique in the world.

Health Care

Health care is another area that falls under the umbrella of American exceptionalism. Health-care in the US is an uncoordinated collection of independent, profit driven companies. Virtually every other industrialized country, has a single, affordable health care system. Although the implementation details differ in each country, the results are the same—everyone has access to health care at no direct cost or at a low, affordable cost. In these other countries, health care is considered to be on the same level with police protection, public education, national security, and Social Security.

It is widely recognized that the cost of health care and drugs and medical equipment and, therefore, insurance is much higher in the US than in any other country. The number 1 reason for bankruptcies in

America is the profit-driven health-care system. Every aspect of health care in the US is highest in the world due to enormous salaries, corporate profits, and unproductive overhead. 62% of all US bankruptcies are due to the enormous expenses of American health care. This is not due to a lack of insurance because 72% of those bankruptcies were by people with insurance[29]. Universal health care benefits the working-class citizens by making it more affordable. There are several reasons that health care is so expensive in the US.

Competition

Normally, free-market competition would provide incentives to keep costs low. However, there is little, if any, competition in the US health-care system. It is next to impossible for the consumer to shop around for the most cost-effective and customer-friendly provider. If your physician sends you to Good Luck Hospital, you don't argue and demand to send out an RFP (request for proposal) to local hospitals asking them for bids on your brain transplant operation. Also, you do not put an ad on Craig's List to interview anesthesiologists or LVNs. Health care does not operate in a competitive free market.

In 2003, Billy Tauzin, a Republican congressman from Louisiana, was the Republican chairman of the House Committee on Energy and Commerce. Billy was given the responsibility of defining the rules in the Medicare Drug Bill.[30] The Republican priority is the profits of the drug companies. They had little concern for the affordability of drugs sold to the public. So Tauzin allowed the drug companies to write the Medicare Drug Bill. That's right—Billy gave the keys to the henhouse to the fox. (See the "Fifth Law of Politics"— Republicans always put interests of the super wealthy ahead of the working class.)

The easiest way to guarantee enormous drug-company profits is to eliminate any obstacles to competitive drug pricing. So that's what the drug company lobbyists did when they wrote the Medicare Drug Bill. This drug company–written bill made it illegal to negotiate for lower drug prices as it is done by the VA hospitals, by HMOs, and by other countries in the world. The Republican bill prevented Medicare drugs from being competitively priced. This is the opposite of what politicians are always preaching—free markets and competition will keep prices down. Yet Republicans outlawed the competitive markets for Medicare drug prices. The drug companies were so grateful to Billy Tauzin for handing them billions of dollars of your money that Tauzin was hired as the chief drug lobbyist at $2 million per year. Yes, thanks to the Republicans, the enormous drug profits and Tauzin's compensation eventually come out of your bank account.

The Medicare Prescription Drug, Improvement, and Modernization Act of 2003 was passed on November 11 of that year. 82% of Republicans voted for the bill that prohibited free-market drug pricing while 76% of Democrats voted against the bill. Ever since then, Americans have been handing over billions of their hard-earned wages to drug companies for no reason other than Republicans voting to ensure their wealthy sponsors would continue giving them campaign money. Republicans talk about free market competition but then did the opposite which raises prices for consumers.

All politicians must be held accountable for their actions. Republican politicians should be held accountable for their decision to suppress the free-market pricing of Medicare drugs[31].

Table 3 shows how drugs are more expensive in the US than in other countries.

Table 3
International Drug Prices

	US	Canada	UK	Spain
Enbrel	$3,000	$1,646	$1,117	$1,386
Celebrex	$330	$51	$112	$164
Copaxone	$3,900	$1,400	$862	$1,191
Gleevec	$8,500	$1,141	$2,697	$3,348
Humira	$3,049	$1,950	$1,102	$1,498

[32]

One of Trump's campaign promises was that he would get drug prices reduced. Many elderly people were happy to hear this so they voted for Trump. On January 31, 2017, President Trump had a meeting with CEOs of pharmaceutical firms and the chairmen of the Pharmaceutical Research and Manufacturers of America. After the meeting, reporters asked Trump about his pledge to open drug sales to the free market. Trump replied, "We are going to have the best drugs ever. We will have so many great drugs you won't believe it." The reporters sang out in a loud chorus, "Huh?" Trump did not want to upset the drug company CEOs, so he did not even bother to bring up drug pricing.

Insurance companies can negotiate prices with drug companies. But Republicans eliminated negotiating for Medicare drugs, so identical drugs are more expensive in America than in other countries. Only in the US are drugs so highly priced.

According to the nonpartisan Center for Responsive Politics, pharmaceutical companies spent $900 million on lobbying between 1998 and 2005— more than any other industry. During the same period, they donated $89.9 million to federal candidates and political parties, giving approximately three times as much to Republicans as to Democrats. According to the Center for Public Integrity, from January 2005 through June 2006 alone, the pharmaceutical industry spent approximately $182 million on federal lobbying. The industry has 1,274 registered lobbyists in Washington. That's a lot more lobbyists than working-class taxpayers have.

Profits

Everything in the US health-care system comes with a profit margin on top of the actual cost. No other country considers the lives of its citizens to be an opportunity to make enormous profits. When profits are the goal of an organization or individual, everything else, such as quality health care, is a lower priority. Sacrifices are made, and corners are cut to maximize profits, not to increase health-care quality.

The astronomical compensation for health-care executives is justified by claiming it is necessary to have the highest-performing managers. But that is not backed up by the facts. It is a well-kept secret that corporate CEO's compensation does not correlate to performance. "Companies that awarded their Chief Executive Officers higher pay incentive levels had below-median returns, based on a sample of 429 large-cap U.S. companies observed from 2005 to 2015"[33].

Table 4
2017 Health-Care CEO Compensation

Ian Read (Pfizer)—$26.17 million
Michael F. Neidorff (Centene)—$25.26 million
Alex Gorsky (Johnson & Johnson)—$22.84 million
Joseph M. Zubretsky (Molina Healthcare)—$19.74 million
Richard A. Gonzalez (AbbVie)—$19.13 million
Giovanni Caforio (Bristol Myers-Squibb)—$18.69 million
David M. Cordani (Cigna)—$17.55 million
Timothy Wentworth (Express Scripts)—$15.90 million
Miles D. White (Abbott Laboratories)—$15.62 million
John F. Milligan (Gilead Sciences)—$15.44 million
Bruce D. Broussard (Humana)—$14.87 million
Stefano Pessina (Walgreens)—$14.67 million
David A. Ricks (Eli Lilly)—$14.50 million
R. Milton Johnson (HCA Healthcare)—$13.71 million
George S. Barrett (Cardinal Health)—$10.99 million
Average—$16 million in 2017 [34]

It is impossible to justify $20 million compensation when $5 million compensation would be just as effective and would provide higher dividends and lower health-care costs. No CEO has ever said, "If I got an additional $10 million in compensation, I would make better decisions." In fact, it is usually the opposite. A CEO does not want to lose his mountains of money, so his attitude is "do nothing to rock the boat." This discourages aggressive, bold decisions required to increase market share and to open new markets necessary for growth and increased share prices. There are many examples of high compensation encouraging conservative management styles that led to falling behind. The near demise of IBM because of conservative decisions regarding the personal-computer business is one of these. Eastman Kodak also suffered from not keeping up with changing times.

As long as the primary goal of health care in the US is to increase profits and they have no real competition, health care will always be stuck with million-dollar salaries and enormous price markups and less-than-optimum health care for Americans. The unique American health-care system is perhaps the worst part of American exceptionalism.

Overhead

Administration of all the disparate policies and programs adds a large layer of administrative overhead to the cost of health care in the US. The administrative overhead is orders of magnitude greater in the US than in other countries.

Health-care administration is incredibly complicated due to all the many ways health care is paid to providers. The US has a plethora of insurance companies and programs, government programs, and countless provider policies and guidelines. It takes an army of clerical employees and mountains of forms to manage and coordinate this complex administration. The medical-billing work is so complicated it requires nearly one year of specialized training and certification in medical billing and coding. Medical-coding employees earn about 24 dollars per hour and about $50,000 per year, depending on the location.

The US Government Accountability Office concluded, "If we could get administrative costs of our medical system down to the Canadian level, the money saved would be enough to pay for health care for all the Americans who are uninsured."

The last thing anyone making big bags of money in the American health-care system wants is changes in this antiquated system. To make sure no changes are made, they cut the politicians in on the action big time as noted above. They also pour truckloads of dollars into promoting the idea that any kind of government involvement in health care is automatically a disaster resulting in terrible service and delays.

Other Problems

These problems could have been minimized with the government-insurance option that was proposed for inclusion in the Affordable Care Act. But Republicans, who attack all government services as inefficient, refused to even consider a public-option alternative. They argued that a government-insurance option would be so efficient and cost-effective that it would drive the for-profit insurance companies out of business and insurance would become more affordable for Americans. If you are not paying attention, you should read that last sentence over again. The party that claims all government operations are wasting money rejected the public-insurance option because it would be too *cost*-effective. "Republicans unanimously oppose the government-run insurance option, saying it would drive private insurers from the market"[35].

Table 5

Health Care Quality of Service by Country

	Australia	Germany	New Zealand	United Kingdom	United States
Overall Ranking	3.5	2	3.5	1	6
Quality Care	4	2.5	2.5	1	5
Right Care	5	3	4	2	1
Safe Care	4	1	3	2	6
Coordinated Care	3	4	2	1	5
Patient-Centered Care	3	2	1	4	5
Access	3	1	2	4	6
Efficiency	4	3	2	1	6
Equity	2	4	3		6
Healthy Lives	1	2	4.5	4.5	6
Cost per Capita	$2,876	$3,005	$2,083	$2,546	$6,102

(1 = highest ranking)[36]

Another untruthful charge by conservatives is that people in countries with universal health care are very dissatisfied with their health care. Republicans tell us universal health care is terrible because taxes would go up and services would go down. They never mention that your insurance and medical costs would go down. The truth is that people in other countries are happier with their health-care systems than Americans are. Survey data (before Obamacare) of health-care satisfaction in other countries show how poorly the US is rated compared to other countries. Table 5 shows that people in Germany have the highest level of satisfaction with their universal health-care system.

Why do Republicans keep scaring the public with false claims about the poor service inherent in public health care? The only rational answer is that Republicans do not want to lose the highly profitable, overpriced health-care system we have today. Health care cost Americans much more than it does people in other countries, yet Americans are much less satisfied with their health care than are people in other countries.

An American Sickness by Elisabeth Rosenthal is an excellent book that goes into detail about the many pharmaceutical and hospital scams that are employed to increase their profits. Rosenthal discusses the high price of a drug promoted as new and improved when it is chemically the same as an existing drug. She discusses how doctors can get paid for "participating" in procedures carried out simultaneously in different locations. Rosenthal also tells about how bacillus Calmette-Guerin (BCG), a cheap generic drug, was effective in reducing or curing type 1 diabetes but was rejected by companies with big incomes in the diabetes industry because they could not make enough profit from it. The bottom line is that if you need good, affordable health care, you should try Germany or England (see tables 3, 4, and 5).

As long as profits are the top priority of the health-care industry, high-quality, affordable health care is a lower priority. Profits are always number 1. The lack of affordable universal health care is one of the hallmarks of American exceptionalism. The primary obstacle to more competitive and affordable health care in the US is the Republicans and conservatives who work with the industry to game the system.

Handguns

The US has many more per capita gun deaths than any other developed country, and this must be included as part of American exceptionalism.

Statistics in The Week, magazine, October 27, 2017

- Every day 300 Americans are shot.
- Every day two women are fatally shot by their partners.
- 6,000 children are shot each year (1,200 accidentally, 1,300 fatally).
- 81 mass gun-killing events (more than three killed) since 1982.
- The year 2015 was a typical year with 36,252 gun deaths and 85,000 gun injuries.
- More Americans have been killed by other Americans with guns than have been killed in all the US wars in history.

By any measure, these numbers are shocking, yet even more shocking is that conservative politicians refuse to do anything to address this problem. The National Rifle Association (NRA) has convinced gun people of the amazingly illogical belief that there would be less gun killings if everyone had a gun. Never mind that most mass gun shooters don't care if they get shot and frequently shoot themselves or that thousands are shot by accident or by mistake.

1200 children have been murdered with guns since the 2018 massacre at Parkland Florida[37], and yet Republicans refuse to even recognize this is a problem.

To deflect any limits on guns, the National Rifle Association (NRA) always talks about the need for protection from burglars and muggers. The NRA never talks about all the deaths that are not associated with crimes. Thousands are shot and killed every year by people who are not criminals.

Gun killings not by criminals
- —accidents
- —mistakes
- —road rage
- —jealous spouses
- —children playing with guns
- —disturbed students
- —angry employees
- —"unloaded" guns

This writer had five personal acquaintances killed in five separate events by shooters who were not criminals.

It is a statistical fact and simple common sense that

- more cars = more car accidents and
- more guns = more gun shootings.

The states with the most guns have the most gun deaths per capita (chart 3).

Public Opinion

The American public is almost unanimous—90%—in demanding background checks for all gun sales. Yet 100% of all Republicans in Washington voted against background checks[38]. Most Americans—70%—want assault-style weapons banned as they have been in the past. Yet Republicans in Washington have refused to address the subject of assault-style weapons or any sensible gun legislation. Republicans are terrified that the National Rifle Association will attack them in primary elections, so they do whatever the NRA tells them to do.

This is not the way representative government is supposed to work. So the slaughter of thousands of Americans, including innocent little children, will continue unabated indefinitely until Democrats and all concerned Americans can overcome the NRA strangle hold on Republicans. (See the "Fourth Law of Politics"— Republicans refuse to address the 30,000 annual gun deaths.)

Chart 3
Number of Guns vs. Number of Gun Deaths

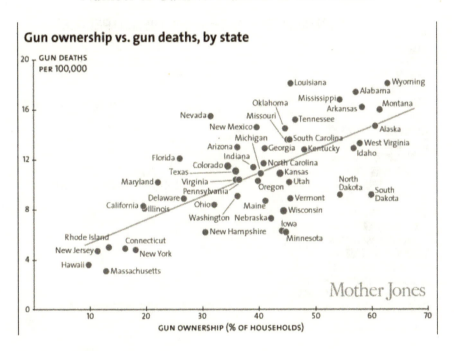

Source: *Mother Jones*

Chart 4
Gun Deaths by Country

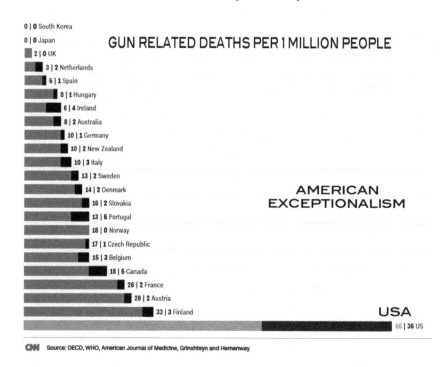

Source: https://www.thedailybeast.com/nearly-1200-us-kids-dead-from-guns-since-parkland-massacre-report

The enormous number of gun deaths in the US is a big reason people in other countries do not want to immigrate to, or even visit, the USA. People in Europe see reports of mass shootings in the USA every few weeks, and they are amazed and bewildered why Americans consider this normal and acceptable. They see reports of 20 six-year-old schoolchildren being murdered, and they are outraged and confused as to how anyone can think this is OK. They see videos of police routinely murdering unarmed citizens, and they are happy they do not live in such treacherous country. People around the world believe there is something seriously wrong with Americans who treasure their handguns and machine guns above everything else.

> The Second Amendment reads, "A well-regulated Militia, being necessary to the security of a free State, the right of the people to keep and bear Arms, shall not be infringed."

The Second Amendment is clearly about defending the state against enemies of the people— either foreign or federal. The Second Amendment was needed to enable citizens to fight against hostile forces because at the time the country had no standing army and did not anticipate having one.

The Brown Bess musket used in 1776 was the state of the art in guns and could not fire more than four bullets per minute[39]. To wage any kind of war, opponents need adequate arms. Handguns provide no resistance to an army that has thousands of bomber drones or Tomahawk missile submarines. So any laws prohibiting citizens from owning an Abrams battle tank is unconstitutional. A municipal law is unconstitutional if it prohibits Walmart from selling military flamethrowers. Of course, this is absurd, but that's exactly the intent of the Second Amendment. Conservatives and others are always insisting that we must observe the Constitution as it was originally intended and not misinterpret it by activist judges. In a rational, logical world, we would either properly enforce the Second Amendment or repeal it.

Someday the courts will uphold the original intent of the Second Amendment and rule that laws prohibiting citizens from owning SAM missile launchers are unconstitutional. Gun killings are another example of American exceptionalism.

PART FIVE

Beyond the Headlines

As democracy is perfected, the office of the President represents, more and more closely, the inner soul of the people. On some great and glorious day, the plain folks of the land will reach their heart's desire at last, and the White House will be occupied by a downright fool and a complete narcissistic moron.

—H.L. Mencken, July 26, 1920

It is the job of the mainstream media to report the day's events and the current issues of interest. The long-term perspective and backgrounds are rarely mentioned on the six-o'clock news. This part looks at items not usually covered in the daily media.

Democrat and Republican Economies

It is a little understood fact that the economy has done better under Democrats. (See charts 5 and 6.)

A major misunderstanding in American politics involves the economy. Polls often show that, contrary to all the evidence, most people believe Republicans are better at managing the economy than Democrats. They are not. All the economic indicators—GDP (gross domestic product), S&P (Standard & Poor's), deficits, profits, jobs, incomes, etc.—have historically been better under Democratic administrations.

In the July 29, 2014 issue of Fortune magazine the paper released by the National Bureau of Economic Research was discussed. The paper was the work of Princeton economists Alan Binder and Mark Watson. Their research showed that there was a "startling large" difference in economic growth between Democratic administrations and Republican administrations.[40]

In Fortune magazine Chris Matthews wrote about the study by the Princeton economists.

> While hardly a secret, it is not nearly as widely known as it should be: The economy grows notably faster when a Democrat is president than when a Republican is.
> The U.S. economy performs much better when a Democrat is president than when a Republican is. The U.S. economy not only grows faster, according to real GDP and other measures, during Democratic versus Republican presidencies, it also produces more jobs, lowers the unemployment rate, generates higher corporate profits and investment, and turns in higher stock market returns. Indeed, it outperforms under all standard macroeconomic metrics. By some measures, the partisan performance gap is startlingly large—so large, in fact, that it strains credulity, given how little influence over the economy most economists (or the Constitution, for that matter) assign to the President of the United States[41].

Forbes magazine[42]

- Stock markets do better under Democrat presidents than Republican presidents.

- Nine of the last ten recessions have occurred under Republican presidents.
- Democratic presidents create nearly twice as many jobs per year as Republican presidents.
- Republican presidents' deficits are 25% larger than Democrats' and 63% higher as a percent of GDP.
- GDP grows 44% faster under Democratic presidents.
- Business investment has grown twice as fast under Democratic presidents than under Republican presidents.

This misunderstanding is generally attributed to the Republican strategy of being on an offensive attack mode at all times even when no elections are imminent. After an election, Democrats go into election hibernation, allowing the Republican machine to storm ahead unimpeded. When a Democrat is in the White House, Republicans constantly tell their base they are suffering horribly because of Democrats, whether or not they really are. Democrats counter back with silent smiles and polite denials. Then they gather together and agree they lost the election because they were too aggressive.

Chart 5
GDP Growth by Party

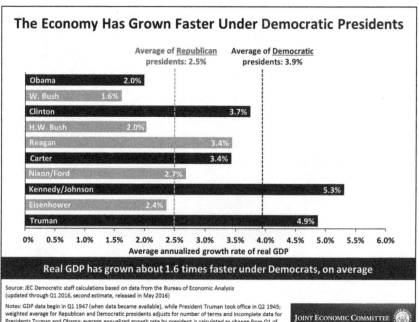

Chart 6
Job Growth by Party

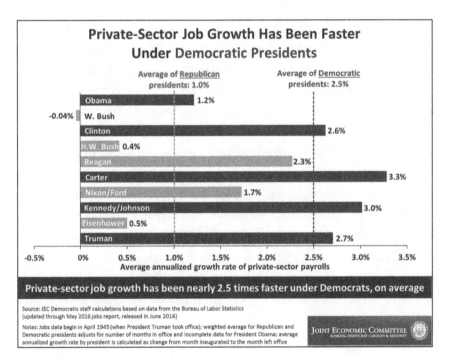

Of course, Republicans will deny that the economy is better under Democrats and come up with creative excuses to explain the one-sided data. But unbiased, independent, objective analyses always show it is an undeniable fact that the economy does better under the Democrats. (See the "Second Law of Politics"—the economy does better under Democrats than under Republicans.)

Regulations

It is an established economic principle that completely unregulated capitalism eventually leads to enormous swings between boom and bust fueled by high speculation. It also leads to extreme differences in wealth and income and to the loss of the middle class. But perhaps the most devastating product of unregulated capitalism is the inevitable emergence of monopolies. The day after doughnuts become a monopoly product, the price would suddenly jump from $1.70 per doughnut to $4.90 per doughnut. Excessive, unnecessary regulations also have problems, but proper regulations provide a sensible throttle avoiding economic extremes.

The two most devastating economic collapses occurred under Republican presidents and policies— the Great Depression of 1929 (Coolidge) and the Great Recession of 2008 (G. W. Bush). Both crashes were in part due to uncontrolled, high-risk stock market speculations. To avoid a repetition of the crash of 1929 and the corresponding failure of 5,000 banks, the Democratic Congress passed the Glass-Steagall Act in 1933.

Glass-Steagall prohibited commercial banks from engaging in highly speculative activities using public deposits. Glass-Steagall required investment banking to be separated from commercial banking. Investment banks were prohibited from taking consumer deposits. They were also restricted from using consumer deposits that were in commercial banks. This way, customer savings accounts would be protected from stock market crashes and from the speculative gambling practices of banks. It forced banks to lose the bank's money instead of depositor's money when their speculations generated enormous loses.

66 years later, Republicans were able to get Glass-Steagall repealed. All 54 Republican senators voted to repeal Glass-Steagall. All 44 Democrat senators voted to keep the constraints on bank speculations. This repeal played a significant role in the events leading to the Great Recession of 2008 during the Republican administration of George W. Bush.

Wall Street investment banks put together confusing, complicated mortgage-backed security (MBS) packages called tranches[43] and derivatives[44]. Also bankers traded investment insurances called credit default swaps that were thought to be more secure than they really were[45]. These packages were so confusing that nobody knew what their actual value was. Investment bankers with their million-dollar salaries did not understand what they were doing. It was all just blind speculation. Playing craps at a gambling casino was safer and made more sense. When these investments turned out to be worthless in 2008, Lehman Brothers went bankrupt and 450 smaller banks around the country also failed like they did in 1929.

The MBSs contained variable interest loans that were being paid without problems until the variable rates were increased. These new interest rates led to foreclosures and dropping home values. With the drop in real estate, the packages could not be traded. This triggered a chain reaction throughout the financial industry that resulted in one of the greatest recessions in US history. This speculative system did not exist before Republicans got Glass-Steagall repealed.

Experienced economists sat around a big mahogany table and agreed that the Republicans should not have repealed Glass-Steagall. Republican/Libertarian Allen Greenspan, who was chairman of the Federal Reserve for 19years and a strong fiscal conservative, admitted in a Senate hearing that repealing the Glass-Steagall Act was a major cause of the 2008 Great Recession and was a big mistake. There were other factors involved in these economic collapses, but Republican-sponsored deregulation was a major factor.

More large banks would also have failed if the government had not stepped in and lent them money. In spite of these disastrous, irresponsible behaviors by the banks, none of the bank executives went to jail and they continued to collect million-dollar bonuses. Meanwhile, the irresponsible actions of the Republicans caused millions of working-class Americans to lose their homes and were forced to live in their SUVs.

The Great Recession of 2008 was a stark reminder of why the Glass-Steagall Act was passed in 1933. It was evident to everyone that a Glass-Steagall type of regulation was needed again. Democrats, with minimal Republican support, passed the Dodd-Frank Act in 2010. This was a modified version of the old Glass-Steagall Act. This act restored the limits on bank speculations and established the Consumer Financial Protection Bureau (CFPB). However, as soon as Republicans regained control of the House in 2017, they voted to repeal the Dodd-Frank bill just as they repealed Glass-Steagall in 2010. Apparently, Republicans had not learned the lessons of 1929 or 2008.

Removing Consumer Protections

The Consumer Financial Protection Bureau (CFPB) helps level the playing field so that the typical working-class consumer is not at the mercy of the professionals who can easily take advantage of consumers by manipulating agreements and loans to their advantage. For example, loan companies have illegally charged 900% interest rates that are hidden in the small print in loan contracts. This type of fiscal fraud has destroyed people's lives.

The CFPB sets guidelines for loans such as the maximum debt-to-income ratio - 43%. It also provides a process to file complaints against banks and financial institutions. These complaints have resulted in $12 billion returned to 29 million consumers and imposed about $600 million in civil penalties. The CFPB has also created information sources to help consumers understand financial issues and to help determine the cost of attending specific universities based on the financial aid a student is considering.

Republicans oppose banking regulations and consumer protections with the same vigor and determination they oppose health-care programs and background checks. For example, Trump appointed Mick

Mulvaney to be the director of the CFPB. Mulvaney was opposed to the CFPB and to all its consumer protections. Mulvaney stopped the legal actions against criminal loan sharks from proceeding.

Mulvaney and Trump proposed to eliminate consumer protections from the 2018 budget. Mulvaney and Trump were disappointed to learn that the CFPB is not funded through the budget. It is funded by the Federal Reserve. So Republican efforts to eliminate consumer protections have been foiled. However, Mulvaney was successful in dropping several high-profile lawsuits against predatory payday lenders. He also dropped an investigation into a lender that contributed directly to Mulvaney's campaign.

One of these predatory lenders was Golden Valley Lending owned by an American Indian tribe in California. This lender was charging up to 950% interest and was in violation of lending laws in 17 states. CFPB had spent many months building up the case against Golden Valley Lending and had a very strong case. Republican Mulvaney believes it is OK for lenders to practice criminal levels of predatory lending and to hide it in the tiny print of lending agreements. So Mulvaney, to the shock and frustration of the CFPB staff, had the case against Golden Valley dropped. (See the "Fifth Law of Politics"—Republicans always put interests of the superwealthy ahead of the working class.)

Regardless of what Republicans say in public, the truth is that Republicans have always opposed consumer protections and have always opposed regulations on risky speculations by banks.

Economic Evolution

Communism was tried and failed. Unregulated capitalism was tried and failed. These painful trial-and-error experiments have taught the world that the most consistently successful economic system is a properly regulated socialism-capitalism system. Every democratic country today employs a properly regulated capitalist system that has elements of socialism such as public schools, universal health care, social security, and consumer protections. Even communist China has integrated regulated capitalism into its economy. We have tried the extremes and learned that a middle road of moderation is the best overall system. The successful economies in the twenty-first century incorporate parts of socialism and capitalism that benefit both the wealthy and the working class.

Rise and Fall of Communism

The twentieth century was a century of political/government experiments. We learned that communism does not work and that unregulated capitalism does not work. If you step back and look at the big picture, you see a pattern.

In 1900 Russia, the working class was starving and living in tiny apartments and dying from a variety of diseases. Meanwhile, the ruling class was dining and dancing in elaborate homes and palaces. Uprisings in 1905 were put down by shooting hundreds of demonstrators, including women and children. Eventually, the working class became so desperate they rebelled and killed the czar and his family. The revolutionaries embraced communism as preferable to a monarchy with a small superwealthy class. Then in 1988, communism was dropped and a system of capitalistic socialism was adopted.

In 1950 Cuba, conditions were similar to those of 1900 Russia. The working class could barely survive on the minimal wages they were paid while the wealthy class was earning millions from their sugar plantations. Uprisings in 1956 were put down by shooting 20,000 civilians. Eventually, the working class became so desperate they rebelled in 1959 and defeated President Batista's army. The revolutionaries embraced communism as preferable to a very corrupt dictator with a small superwealthy class. In 1996, communism was modified to include some capitalism. It is continuing to expand capitalism today.

The French Revolution, Chinese Revolution, and other revolutions have followed similar patterns:

1. The superwealthy exploits the exploitable.
2. The starving, suffering, subsident class starts a revolution.

3. The rebels go all the way over to the extreme opposite economic anticapitalism system in an overreaction to the severe living conditions they endured.
4. Eventually, the anticapitalism communism has problems.
5. The people back off total communism and move toward a blend of controlled capitalism and limited socialism.

The policy of the people owning all production and property was very appealing to oppressed people. People readily joined the communist movement out of desperation for a better life. They could not have anticipated that communism would fail because it stifled progress and innovation.

Communism was inevitable due to the super rich refusing to recognize the problem of the starving millions and doing nothing to help them. We have gone down both extreme paths and ended up in the middle.

Few billionaire-capitalist understand that the foundation of success is a thriving, stable working class. This could be called bubble-up economics.

Rise and Fall of Unregulated Capitalism

Nearly everyone in America, regardless of party, believes in and supports capitalism. There are virtually no communists or Marxists in the US, even though the radio ranters carry on as if communists are lurking around every corner. This incredible nonsense appeals to a surprisingly large portion of voters, especially to conservatives who are naturally more paranoid than the general population and susceptible to conspiracy accusations.

The real economic world is more complicated than either capitalism or communism. While communism has generally been unsuccessful, the Chinese version of communism is now doing well after going through periods of difficulty. Capitalism has also had periods of difficulty.

Unregulated capitalism was embraced in countries where there was a thriving middle class free of exploitation by a ruling class. But like communism, it was difficult to anticipate the problems.

The historical record is clear. There are three main problems with out-of-control, unregulated capitalism.

1. It inevitably results in extreme swings from rapid inflation to sudden widespread unemployment.
2. It invariably leads to monopolies. A monopoly is the ultimate prize in capitalism. The lack of competition gives a company license to increase prices and profits indiscriminately.
3. It eventually evolves into extreme income inequality between a superwealthy leisure class and a struggling, underpaid working class.

A famous example of a yo-yo economy was the great Dutch Tulip Bulb Mania of 1636. In just three months (from November 12, 1636, to February 3, 1637), the price of certain varieties of tulip bulbs skyrocketed from just a few dollars to as much as $25,000. People were making fortunes every day. Ordinary working people traded all their farm animals and possessions for a single Viceroy-variety tulip bulb. Then on February 3, the market suddenly collapsed; and in a few days, tulip bulbs were back to only a few dollars. Thousands lost everything they had[46].

Another noteworthy example of the problems with unregulated capitalism is the US onion market in 1955. Two onion traders managed to get control of the entire onion production that year. They then were able to manipulate the price of onions. The traders made millions of dollars, while many farmers went bankrupt. In reaction to this, Congress passed a law making it illegal to speculate in onions. This remains the only prohibition against the speculations in farm products.

Speculation was the same mechanism that contributed to the Great Depression of 1929 and the Great Recession of 2008. Inexperienced people do not consider the possibility of a sudden collapse of a supersaturated market. The only thing they focus on is easily getting a lot of money. Despite these common sense lessons, Republicans continue to oppose business regulations that put limits on speculations.

Monopolies always lead to excessive, unjust disparities between the working class and the wealthy ruling class. Unregulated capitalism eventually leads to a small superwealthy group and a large population of impoverished workers. Table 6 illustrates countries and their GINI index, where 0 is complete equality and 100 is total inequality. The US is ranked 92 out of 154 countries. This means there are 91 countries with more income equality than the US[47].

Table 6
Income Equality by Country—GINI Index

Rank out of 154 Countries	Country	GINI Index
10	Finland	27.1
11	Sweden	27.3
18	Denmark	29.1
22	Germany	30.1
38	United Kingdom	32.6
42	France	33.1
51	India	33.9
55	Australia	34.9
57	Italy	35.2
92	**United States**	**41.1**
93	Russia	41.6
95	China	42.1
132	Mexico	48.1

100 = no income equality at all

Increasing inequality results from an economy that is a positive feedback system. In plain English, this means that the presence of income inequality is the fuel that causes income inequality to increase even more. Think of your car's cruise control system. Like all control systems, it is a negative feedback system. When the car's speed increases above the target speed, the fuel feed system decreases slightly until the speed decreases back to the target speed. An unregulated, out-of-control capitalism system has no negative feedback mechanism.

So when corporate profits surge, the increase in profits is directed toward increasing profits even more without regard to any impact to consumers or safety or inflation. Like a car without negative feedback, the engine keeps racing faster and faster until it blows up.

Trickle Down

Republicans want you to believe that trickle-down policies are good for the working class. This is the theory whereby the top-income brackets receive big tax breaks, and these tax handouts are justified by claiming they will spur investments that create jobs. They do not tell the voters that there is no evidence to prove that tax cuts for the wealthy creates jobs for the working class. In reality, it is just a way to repay their wealthy campaign contributors.

This is also referred to as supply-side economics, which holds that supply creates demand. In some markets, supply can contribute to demand; however, demand is usually the independent variable affecting supply and not the other way around. If buyers have very little money to spend, all the supply in the world does not increase sales. When inventory supplies greatly exceeds demands, the imbalance can trigger economic instability and crashes.

Economists have invoked advanced mathematics along with empirical data to study the correlations between supply and demand. Sometimes a new product can create a demand that had not existed previously. This was the case with smartphones and with personal computers.

Usually, demand drives supply and not the reverse. Producing more bicycles does not create a consumer demand to own more bicycles. The average voter is not experienced enough to see through this con game, so they just assume the politicians would never tell them something that is not true. They are mollified into trusting that the politicians will do the right thing for them.

There are lots of examples of failures of the trickle-down/supply-side theories. One recent example of the failure of trickle down is the state of Kansas. Republican governor Brownback implemented tax cuts for the wealthy and for corporations in 2012. He promised this would create jobs and produce a surge in the state economy. The opposite happened. Kansas was forced to slash education funding, reduce basic services like maintenance of roads and bridges, and deal with large budget shortages. Bloomberg columnist Justin Fox described this disaster in his 2017 article:

> Kansas lags its economically similar neighbors in nearly every major category: job creation, unemployment, gross domestic product, and taxes collected. Pretty much across the board, the gap between Kansas and nearby states has widened, and it has been getting even wider lately.

Brownback kept defending the Kansas fiscal policy by saying, "It takes time to be effective." After five years of waiting for it "to be effective," many Kansas Republicans finally admitted that lowering taxes for the wealthy created a recession, so they joined the Democrats in opposing Brownback and voted in 2017 to scrap their disastrous trickle-down fiscal plan. Citizens in Kansas have experienced the false myth of tax cuts the hard way. Both parties in Kansas have since moved to repeal the tax cuts[48].

The failed Republican fiscal policies in Kansas helps to explain why the US economy has done better under Democratic administrations than under Republican administrations. Republican policies are directed toward benefitting millionaires and billionaires. Further proof of this is the Republican revised tax laws in 2018 and the attempt to replace the Affordable Care Act with a program tailored to benefit the wealthy health care moguls.

In spite of real-world empirical evidence to the contrary, Republicans continue to tell the working class how great everything will be as soon as the superwealthy billionaires get more money.

On the other hand California raised taxes. Raising taxes did not slow down the continuing growth of the dynamic California economy. For the fiscal year 2017, growth rate was 2.6% in California and only 1% in Kansas[49]. The per capita GDP of California in 2017 was $60,000 per person, while in Kansas, it was only $47,000 per person[50].

Budget cuts in the Republican-controlled states of West Virginia, Kentucky, Oklahoma, and Arizona led to massive teacher walkouts and closed schools in 2018. Highly educated teachers could barely support their families and many have been forced to get part-time jobs at McDonald's or Walmart. These Republican states have reconsidered the actual consequences of trickle-down budgets[51].

Republicans insisted that the Bush tax cuts in 2001 and 2003 would create jobs and create a booming economy. It never happened. In fact, the unemployment rate before the Bush tax cuts was only 4%. At the end of Bush's term in 2008, the unemployment rate was over 10% and kept on increasing the first few months of the Obama administration. The Bush tax cuts may have helped to create the Great Recession of 2008.

Yet in spite of all the evidence to the contrary, Republicans continue to preach that giving more free money to billionaires is good for the working class. And that's exactly what they did with their federal tax rates in 2018. This gift to billionaires did nothing to spur the economy that was already doing well. Giving tax money to billionaires contributes to income inequality, greatly increases the national debt, and does nothing to increase jobs or opportunities.

As a result of the Trump tax cuts for the rich, the national debt is projected to increase by $2.3 trillion in the next decade. The national debt in 2018 is about $15 trillion, or 78% of GDP (gross domestic product). This debt is projected to increase to 113% of GDP in 30 years⁽⁵²⁾. This is the largest debt since the record debt created by World War II and the Great Depression combined. Such a large debt can lead to the US unable to deal with emergencies and recessions. It can lead to reduced individual incomes and paying higher interest to international money markets.

When Obama was president, the Tea Party branch of the Republican Party strongly objected to increasing the national debt. The Tea Party was highly vocal all across the country and marched on Washington in 2009. They demanded a smaller budget and a decrease in the national debt. They expected President Trump to address their concerns regarding the national debt. But Trump's tax plan did the opposite. The Tea Party said nothing. Apparently, they did not mind a much greater national debt as long as it was created by a Republican president.

Republicans faced a dilemma. A major tenet of conservative beliefs is small government without unnecessary debts. But Trump, the Republican leader, was responsible for an enormous increase in debt. Republicans had to choose between their core belief of fiscally responsible government or the president who had consistently low approval ratings across the country. They reluctantly gave up their policy of small government and continued to support the unpopular president. It is clear that many people consider themselves to be Republicans first and Americans second.

The reason the stock market had been going up ever since 2009 during the Obama administration is that most companies are making good profits and have large cash reserves. They are not waiting for big tax breaks so they could create more jobs. They have more than enough money to hire workers at any time. Apple Company is now worth $1 trillion, which is a historical world record.

So what will corporations do with the money that would have gone to taxes? It is not going to end up in the pockets of the working class. Some will go to the millionaire executives, and some will go to the election campaigns of the politicians that gave it to them. And some goes to stockholders. No one expects worker wages to go up.

Minimum Wage

Republicans are always opposed to adjusting the minimum wage for inflation. They claim it will cause the closure of many businesses and hurt the overall economy. That is not true. The minimum wage has been adjusted for inflation many times since it was established in 1938. Raising the minimum wage has never hurt the economy. A small number of employees have been laid off, but the overall effect is that many people no longer had to work two or three jobs. Some families had a little more money, and they spent it on all kinds of consumer goods thereby increasing the demand for products and services, which is what drives the economy.

The great Henry Ford knew this. He said, "Paying good wages is not charity at all—it is the best kind of business. No one loses anything by raising wages as soon as he is able. It has always paid us."

So why do Republicans claim that the effects of adjusting the minimum wage for inflation hurts the economy?

The most obvious answer is that Republicans get more campaign contributions from business owners than they do from hourly employees. Employers naturally want to increase profits, so they must keep all expenses, like wages, as low as possible. Republicans accommodate employers by not requiring cost-of-living adjustments. But politicians are not going to admit that in public, so they have to find something that is acceptable to voters, as if it will cause job losses. This is a successful strategy because no one ever challenges them to prove these false claims. Refusing to adjust the minimum wage for inflation is another example of Republican disregard for the working class.

As long as Republicans are not held accountable for their misleading statements, they will continue to make them. Democrats and the media are afraid to ask Republicans serious, hardball question. America needs a party that is not afraid of challenging false and misleading statement.

The Working Class

After World War II, America enjoyed a period of peace and prosperity. This was portrayed on several TV shows of the time such as *The Adventures of Ozzie and Harriet*. The family always had a father who worked and a mother who stayed at home. They lived in a modest house in a peaceful residential area. They never had any financial problems, rebellious teenagers, or medical emergencies.

Although this is still true of families today, it is almost the exception. Today, usually both parents are working. Often, the parents are divorced. Their jobs have not kept up with the cost of living. Their employers have replaced pension plans with employee-paid 401(k) savings. Company-provided family health-care plans are disappearing. There is little job security, and many college grads have crushing debts and are living with their parents.

It was not surprising that when Donald Trump promised to turn the calendar back to the Ozzie and Harriet days, he was seen as a revolutionary savior. Of course he never did anything like that. The working class was told that their problems were caused by all the minorities—the Mexicans, the Muslims, the Asians, the African Americans, and even the gays. Notice that this dishonest strategy of blaming minority groups for all the problems was also employed in 1935 Germany. They fueled hate and anger by blaming Jews as well as Gypsies and gays. Lies and propaganda worked in 1935, and they work today.

While complete and accurate information is widely available, many prefer to get their information from highly biased sources like Fox News and Rush Limbaugh. These one-sided conservative sources will never talk about how wages, benefits, and job security declined because of the decline in union membership. Charts 7 and 8 show how profits have continued to rise while labor costs remained constant. So owners and investors have been getting ever-increasing profits while the working-class wages have been decreasing after adjustments for inflation.

Unions bargained for layoffs in the order of least seniority. Unions bargained for wages adjusted for inflation. Unions bargained for pension plans and health-care plans. But slowly and over time, Republicans have successfully managed to reduce union membership and union influence in general. At the same time, the extreme-right media have convinced many voters that unions are detrimental to their standard of living. Republicans even got union members to think all problems were due to immigrants. If we want to return to the Ozzie and Harriet days, we should increase union memberships and stop worrying about Mexicans. Unions made America great, not the employers.

Chart 7
Decline in Unions, Decline in Wages

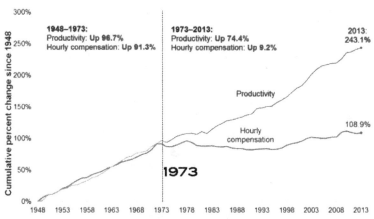

Source: EPI analysis of Bureau of Labor Statistics and Bureau of Economic Analysis data

Chart 8
Decline in Union Membership

Source: https://en.wikipedia.org/wiki/Labor_unions_in_the_United_States [54]

Abortion

Abortion may be the most emotionally charged issue in politics. In 1973, the Supreme Court decided that the state could pass abortion laws regarding pregnancies only for periods past the point of viability—ability to survive outside of the womb—which is after the fifth month. However, antiabortion conservatives believe all abortions, regardless of viability or anything else, should be illegal. The only disagreement is the timing.

When a male spermatozoon joins a female ovum, each with half of a DNA molecule, the two DNA halves combine to form a complete DNA molecule. This is a single-cell zygote, which will continue to grow when each cell divides into two new cells. The zygote is initially formed in the fallopian tube, but after seven days, it becomes embedded in the uterine wall where the zygote continues to grow. That's the way it is supposed to work. In reality, nature does not cooperate 100% of the time.

This summary skips over several complex operations in the complete procedure. For more detailed descriptions, the reader is referred to instructional videos on YouTube. Since this process is delicate and complicated, it often fails, and there are many failed pregnancies. Table 7 shows that many pregnancies are lost before there is even any awareness of the pregnancy [55].

Frequently, these nearly invisible zygotes do not attach to the uterine wall. When that happens, all further growth terminates. Some zygotes do attach to the uterine wall, but then after a few weeks or months, they stop growing and exit the woman's body in the normal course of events.

First-day abortions are opposed on religious beliefs that the moment a female ovum is joined with a male spermatozoon, it is instantly a living human being with an immortal soul. Therefore, in some religions, every termination of a pregnancy, regardless of viability, constitutes murder and must never be allowed. These people should celebrate a person's birthday on the day of conception rather than on the day the umbilical was cut. But of course, they never do.

Table 7

Types of Pregnancy Failures

- Chemical pregnancy
- Ectopic pregnancy
- First-trimester miscarriage
- Blighted ovum
- Missed miscarriage
- Molar pregnancy
- Second-trimester miscarriage
- Preterm delivery from cervical insufficiency loss
- Stillbirth
- Neonatal infant loss
- Termination due to medical reasons

"What Are the Different Types of Pregnancy Loss?" on Verywell Family [55]

The question of abortions due to natural causes or, if you prefer, acts of God are never mentioned by the antiabortion conservatives. All these millions of natural abortions are simply ignored. This presents a dilemma. If abortion of a fertilized egg is murder in violation of divine law, then natural termination must also be a violation of divine law.

For theists, it follows that God chose to terminate a life prior to forming a physical, viable body and that God does this trillions of times for no apparent reason. Based on the religionist definition of *abortion*, God commits many millions of "murders" every year. It defies logic and common sense to think God has some rational reason for committing these trillions of terminations.

The dilemma is that if God can perform abortions, why not humans? The usual refrain is "We cannot understand the mind of God" or something similar. This is strange, irrational behavior by God no matter what your beliefs are. The more common sense belief is that a single-celled zygote has not yet developed into a viable human being with an immortal soul. The Supreme Court decided in 1973 in *Roe v. Wade* that a zygote is not a person until the fourth month.

Pregnancy experts estimate about 50% ± 10% of fertilized eggs end up unborn for various biological reasons (table 7). There are about 350,000 births in the world each day. At 50% that's 350,000 pregnancies terminated naturally by acts of God for a total of 128 million per year (350,000 × 365 ≈ 128,000,000).

A conservative estimate is that over the past hundreds of thousands of years, there have been trillions of naturally failed conceptions. With our advances in medical science, we now have much lower rates of natural pregnancy terminations and infant mortality. But for 99% of the time humans have been around, lost pregnancies and infant mortality were at much higher levels. A very large proportion of two-celled zygotes never made it through pregnancy and infancy. If you are a religious person, you'd believe these terminations were the work of God.

The dilemma is trying to reconcile all the natural deaths and abortions with the belief that abortions are always murder. Those who are adamant about demanding an end to the murder of single-celled zygotes must address the hypocrisy of accepting divine termination of trillions of pregnancies while condemning human termination of pregnancies.

A related question for those who believe a two-celled zygote is a person is, What happens to all those zillions of zygotes that were naturally aborted? Is heaven filled with mountains of two-celled zygotes, or do they acquire adult shapes with intelligence and names and memory? If they truly have souls, then they can't be just tiny collections of idle DNA. Having a life and a soul implies having some sort of intelligence and memory. So after being aborted, do they wake up in heaven fluent in English or Italian and are named Todd or Latisha? Of course, they can't have any memory of life, so the only thing they can know is nothing. They cannot even think of simple things like "Hey, where are my arms and legs?" In other words, they cannot think of anything. This seems like a horrible way to spend eternity and an incredibly severe punishment for a person who has done nothing wrong.

The Catholic Church offers teachings and beliefs regarding unbaptized children but has nothing on unborn infants.

The antiabortion people need to either have answers for these questions or accept the general understanding that a tiny collection of large molecules is not a human being until it develops a heart and a brain. The Bible says nothing on the subject of abortion. So any policies on abortions are just the opinions of mere humans and not the Word of God.

Late-term abortions are a completely different issue.

Global Warming

People who deny the phenomena of global warming are on the conservative side of the street. They seem to have very limited knowledge of the extensive history or the enormous breadth and depth of the science involved. These issues are discussed here to provide a better understanding of the critical subject.

The phenomenon of rising temperatures around planet Earth is not a controversial issue among all the thousands of international scientists or among people who have educated themselves on the subject. The only people who think global warming is a politically driven issue are those unfamiliar with the overwhelming, irrefutable evidence and have been influenced by the campaigns of large oil and coal companies to cast doubt on the science.

The "global warming hoax" promotion is just the latest attempt by corporations to deflect responsibility for various problems away from their products. This has been the standard knee-jerk reaction by large companies ever since there have been large corporations. They do not have to prove that their products are harmless. All they have to do is create a smoke screen of doubt to cultivate confusion about the cause and effect. There are many examples of corporations covering up known problems with their products to maximize profits at the cost of human lives. Here are a few examples.

Leaded Gas

> NEW YORK—The makers of leaded gasoline systematically suppressed information about the severe health hazards of their product for decades, even though they knew from the mid-1920s on that leaded gasoline was a public health menace, according to an investigative article published in the March 20 issue of The Nation. Moreover, both the auto and oil industries, as well as the makers of lead additive, knew from the early 1900s that safe anti-knock substitutes were cheaply available, but rejected them because they would be unprofitable. For years, according to automotive journalist Jamie Kitman, who researched and wrote the article, these manufacturers wildly exaggerated the benefits of leaded gasoline while downplaying or outright denying its dangers. "The story of how millions of tons of lead, a potent neurotoxin, were spewed into the environment and people's blood for 60 years ranks beside tobacco and the exploding gas tank of the Ford Pinto in the annals of corporate crime in America," said Kitman. "And what's truly outrageous, is that leaded gasoline continues to be sold around the world."
>
> —*Lead Action News*, vol. 8 no.1[56]

Lead additives to gasoline were phased out in 1974. A 1985 EPA study estimated that as many as 5,000 Americans had been dying annually from lead-related heart disease before the lead phase-out in the US. The automotive and oil companies knew of the dangers of leaded gasoline but continued to produce it because it helped to maximize profits. No gasoline company executives were charged with murder or any other crime because they said they were sorry and would try to not do it again.

The big health problem cover-up is being repeated today with gasoline lead being replaced by atmospheric carbon dioxide and global warming. The difference is that now we are not looking at the deaths of thousands of people. We are looking at the end of millions of lives, cultures, livelihoods, species, and possibly, global wars unimaginable.

Ford Pinto

The Pinto case is perhaps the best-known example of corporate profiteering overriding public safety and human lives. In 1969, Ford CEO Lee Iacocca directed his engineers to design and build the Pinto car within two years. At the time, a new model car typically required about three to 'five years to design and get into production. The accelerated schedule resulted in some shortcuts and in problems that were not corrected. The biggest problem was the gas tank. The gas tank, at the back of the car, was not protected with a sturdy bumper and would strike two sharp bolts if pushed forward. These problems would cause the gas tank to explode if the car was hit from behind by another car even if it was traveling at a relatively slow speed.

Ford could have made a modification to the car but decided that the cost of the changes was greater than the costs of lawsuits resulting from gas-tank explosions and people burning to death. The problem of people dying was never an issue. It was strictly a profit-analysis decision. Here is a statement describing Ford's policy:

> In the memo, Ford estimated the cost of fuel system modifications to reduce fire risks in rollover events to be $11 per car across 12.5 million cars and light trucks (all manufacturers), for a total of $137 million. The design changes were estimated to save 180 burn deaths and 180 serious injuries per year, a cost to society of only $49.5 million[57].

People were killed in Pinto rear-end collisions. It has been estimated that between 28 and 175 people were killed as a result of the gas-tank problem. The National Highway Traffic Safety Administration (NHTSA) negotiated with Ford to recall and modify the Pintos. Ford managed to drag out the legal process for two years before any action was taken. By that time, the Pinto model was being discontinued. No Ford company executives were charged with murder or any other crime because they said they were sorry and would try not to do it again.

The current obstruction of efforts to reduce global warming is another case of corporations putting profits ahead of the health and safety of human beings.

Cigarette Cancer

In 1994, seven cigarette company executives testified in a congressional hearing that cigarettes were not addictive and did not cause cancer. Even though they were under oath to speak the truth, all these congressional statements were lies. They should have been convicted of perjury and murder, but that would make the executives feel sad, so that was never done. The tobacco companies had known since 1959, from their own internal laboratory studies, that cigarette smoking causes cancer. But they kept this information secret and lied to Congress and to the American people, just like how the oil and coal companies are now lying about global warming.

It is known that cancer is caused by the chemicals in tobacco, specifically by traces of the lethal and radioactive element polonium-210. Tobacco companies knew about polonium as early as 1978, but internal reports were suppressed and never published.

> Polonium-210 in tobacco contributes to many of the cases of lung cancer worldwide. Most of this polonium is derived from lead-210 deposited on tobacco leaves from the atmosphere; the lead-210 is a product of radon-222 gas, much of which appears to originate from the decay of radium-226 from fertilizers applied to the tobacco soils[58].

A decade after a judge ordered tobacco companies to acknowledge the dangers of low-tar cigarettes, they continued to dispute the scientific consensus. Judge Kessler noted that the Justice Department, in a racketeering lawsuit, had presented "overwhelming evidence" of a conspiracy to defraud the public. She ordered the companies to take several actions including ceasing to claim there was such a thing as a low-tar cigarette that reduced the risk of disease.

> In short, tobacco companies have marketed and sold their lethal product with zeal, with deception, with a single-minded focus on their financial success, and without regard for the human tragedy or social costs that success exacted," Kessler wrote in *United States of America v. Philip Morris USA*[59].

Philip Morris ignored the court orders and continued to lie to the public about the health consequences of cigarettes. Philip Morris hired scientists to distort and attack the facts regarding cancer and cigarettes. The "experts" Philip Morris hired worked for companies that specialized in attacking established science and denying any health problems. These companies criticized the other scientists and did whatever they could to establish doubt in the science. In the US, corporations are free to kill people without impunity. No cigarette-company executives were charged with perjury or murder because they said they were sorry and would try not to do it again.

It is a standard practice by corporations to perform a cost-benefit analysis for things that affect their net profits. Oil and gas companies, like the Ford Motor Company, and the cigarette companies have been using this tactic regarding the relationship between CO_2 and global warming.

Naomi Oreskes and Erik M. Conway wrote an outstanding detailed account of the global warming cover-up and other corporate crimes in their book *Masters of Deceit*.

Acid Rain

Another example of an industry attacking and suppressing science are the efforts made by special interests during the Reagan administration to deny the scientific facts of acid rain. There was overwhelming evidence of forests dying off in Canada, the US, and countries like Sweden. There was also irrefutable evidence of freshwater lakes having a pH rating of 4 (a value less than 7 indicates the level of acidity). Through the use of identifying isotopes, this acidity was traced to the SO_2 and NO_2 originating in electric power plants and other emissions. Over the objections of industrial corporations, the Clean Air Act was passed in 1990. In time, this led to the elimination of acid rain and at only a fraction of the cost the industry had been threatening it would cost.

This pattern of industry attacking scientific findings has been repeated regarding ozone depletion, secondhand smoke, catalytic converters, fluoridated water, and now, global warming. In every case, corporations would engage in expensive, broad campaigns to spread misleading information. The sole objective being to make it look like the subject was undecided and surrounded by confusion and doubt when in fact there are no questions or contradictions in the scientific findings. The data on humans causing global warming has been far beyond the slightest doubt for decades.

And yet many social conservatives, including Mr. Trump, continue to deny that global warming is a problem to be concerned about.

Climate Scientists

The findings of the impending global warming disasters are not coming from a handful of political activists. Scientists are ordinary people with families and kids. They just want to go to the ball game and save for their kids' college. Scientists and climate researchers from every country, every university, every military, and hundreds of corporations are all in agreement that the sudden dramatic increase of atmospheric CO_2 over the past 50 years is causing a unique spike in the greenhouse effect resulting in global warming. This is not just their opinion. It is the acceptance of irrefutable data from hundreds of studies and basic research. 97% of scientists agree burning fossil fuels is a major factor causing global warming.[60]

A typical scientist spends many years of intense formal education studying advanced scientific fields of thermodynamics, geology, chemistry, mathematics, physics, tectonics, aerodynamics, hydrodynamics, and statistics. Scientists devote all their time and energy for their entire lives to understanding the processes and the subtle relationships of everything in the natural world. Like most professionals, they take pride in their work and write papers describing their findings. A scientist involved in research is paid to produce factual, repeatable scientific data, findings, and conclusions.

No scientist would dare to stand in front of a group of scientists and present false or biased data. He or she would soon be exposed as a fraud and would be humiliated and ridiculed throughout his community. She would lose the respect of her peers. It is very likely she would lose her job and might be blackballed in the field. Without a job in the field that she studied all her life, she might have to settle for a job at Hooters.

The Great Hoax Conspiracy

It is impossible for the entire world's thousands of climate scientists to suddenly form an enormous clandestine worldwide conspiracy to promulgate an enormous hoax. There is nothing that would motivate all scientists to suddenly go rogue. They have nothing to gain and everything to lose. Scientists are not political operatives. Anyone who thinks otherwise does not understand the world of scientists. Oil company shills came up with the accusation that scientists were lying about their findings so they would get lots of grants. We are still waiting to see evidence of that claim.

The Science

We think of global warming as the increase in atmospheric temperatures. While this is true, it is not the best indicator of global warming. The most significant geophysical indicator among the many metrics is the constant gradual increase in temperature of the world's oceans over the past few decades. The oceans serve as a giant heat sink that retains the planet's heat. Changes in overall ocean temperatures are much slower compared to atmospheric changes. The level of CO_2 in the oceans, as well as the ocean levels, has also been increasing in synchronization with the increase of ocean temperatures and with the increase in atmospheric CO_2.

Oceans are just one of the indicators of global warming. There are many more—such as the shrinking of the North Pole ice cap, the increasing global temperatures, the shrinking coral reefs, rising sea levels, and the shifting locations of flora and fauna.

Global warming will increase as the population increases. Table 8 below shows the breakdown of the human contribution to global warming[61].

Table 8

Global Warming Components

Contributions to Global Warming	
Transportation	14.80%
Manufacturing & Construction	13.30%
Agriculture	11.10%
Wood & Other Fuels	8.20%
Industrial Processes	5.70%
Deforestation	5.70%
Fugitive Emissions	5.30%
Landfill Waste Methane	3.10%
Bunker fuels	2.20%
Total	100.00%

Denial

For several years, the deniers have insisted there is no global warming. Gradually, they have come to accept that global warming is a reality. However, now they insist there is nothing we can do to stop it. Now they are saying this is a natural process that has occurred in the past. This is how the oil and gas companies plant seeds of doubt.

The fluctuations in planet temperatures over the past epochs have been thoroughly studied. In geological time, the temperature changed gradually over thousands of years and not over a few decades as it is currently doing. When a meteor hit our planet 65 million years ago, the effect was cataclysmic. The climate and weather changed rapidly, and all life on the planet was altered. Species died off and were replaced by new species of life. Something similar could happen with the sudden increase in CO_2. Some species and important coral reefs are already dying out.

The oil companies have come up with various reasons why we cannot do anything about global warming: It's due to sunspots, it's due to volcanoes, models are wrong, and so on. A website[62] has been dedicated to addressing every one of these objections. That website has 200 different objections to global warming discussed in detail. Many are discussed at three levels: basic, intermediate, and advanced. Anyone with a sincere interest in understanding all the issues of global warming should go to this site to get the latest, accurate, and complete information.

Consequences

The consequences of ignoring this problem include lost coastal cities and the disappearance of low islands from rising sea levels, more frequent and disastrous weather, increases in heat-related mortalities, increased ocean acidity and all its ramifications, species extinctions, and farming disruptions and relocations.

We are already witnessing some of these problems. Two category 5 hurricanes (Harvey and Irma) smashed into the United States within three weeks in 2017. This has never happened in recorded history. Historical heat records are being set every year around the world. And yet some with no scientific expertise say this is just a coincidence or it's a normal process of balancing the energy distribution. The billions of dollars in damages caused by these global warming catastrophes will be paid by Americans with increased taxes, insurance premiums, and reconstructions.

Before the Industrial Revolution, the CO_2 level was 280 parts per million (ppm). It is now 410 ppm, which is the highest level in the last million years.[63] It is extrapolated to reach 500 ppm in about 30 years. Atmospheric CO_2 has not been that high since the Pliocene epoch 3 million years ago. When that happens, life may cease to exist or at least be greatly changed between the latitudes of Tropics of Cancer and Capricorn.

Normally, nobody would care what the deniers of global warming believe, but they have gained a disproportionate amount of political power in determining the future of our home planet. President Trump has shown no interest in learning anything about global warming. The carbon fuel companies tell Fox News that global warming is not a problem to worry about. Trump believes Fox News TV propaganda pushers and not the scientists.

In April 2016, 195 countries came to a unanimous agreement (a miraculous accomplishment itself) at the UN Paris Convention on Climate Change to voluntarily take steps to reduce CO_2 emissions and global warming. Under Obama, the US was a leader in accomplishing this critical and unanimous decision. A major goal of Trump and Republicans is to reverse everything Obama did regardless of pros and cons or the needs of Americans. Trump decided to prohibit the US from cooperating in reducing global warming even though he has no understanding of global warming. The only thing Trump knows is that Obama agreed with all the other countries. This is not government; it is just revenge politics. (See the "Sixth Law of Politics"—Republicans put party ahead of country.)

Trump believes the oil companies' accusations that global warming is a hoax and that it is not caused by the constant pouring of CO_2, a greenhouse gas, into the atmosphere. Oil companies, like cigarette companies and car companies in the past, are motivated by profits and are unconcerned about collateral damage caused by their products. Science is motivated only by exploring the nature of the world we inhabit. Oil and coal companies have no credibility regarding global warming. Scientists have no conflicts of interests or motivation to distort the facts. In spite of this, Republicans and Trump trust the corporations and do not trust scientists.

Trump's refusal to accept the established science and the resolution of all the countries in the world was met with shock and disbelief by states, by corporations, and by cities across America. Dozens of Fortune 500 companies will ignore Trump's irresponsible decision and will follow the Paris Agreement that requires reductions in greenhouse gas emissions. 14 US states (at the time of writing), which together form the third largest economy in the world, will also ignore Trump's disastrous decision.[64]. The US military branches are proceeding with their preparations to deal with global warming. Hundreds of cities have also agreed to join the rebellion against the conservative efforts to ignore global warming—the second most serious problem of the twenty-first century (the first is overpopulation).

Chart 9
Greenhouse Gas Accumulation

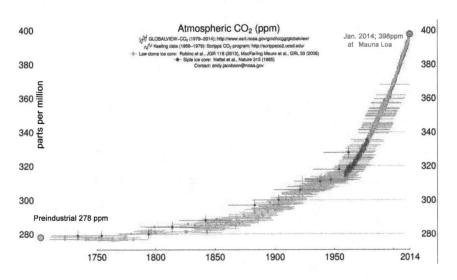

Source: https://www.esrl.noaa.gov/gmd/ccgg/globalview/

Chart 10
Sea Level Rise

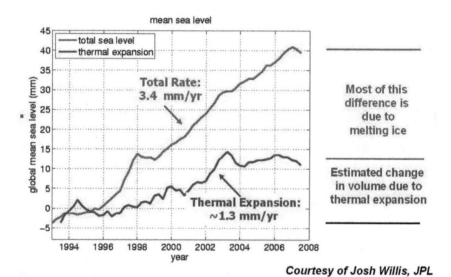

Courtesy of Josh Willis, JPL

Democrats Must Go on the Offense

During an October 2016 presidential debate, Donald Trump said to Hillary Clinton, his opponent, "If I am elected, you'll be in jail." He always called her Crooked Hillary. Hillary had no reply.

This exchange marked the end of the 2016 presidential campaign.

Hillary had shown that she did not know how to fight back against the torrent of lies. She was not prepared or willing to aggressively attack Trump the way he attacked her. Everyone wants a leader who does not roll over and give up. Hillary surrendered like the Iraqi Army did in 2003 to a CNN reporter. She should have stared at him and, in a forceful voice, exposed to the world his long rap sheet of frauds, failures, bankruptcies, scams, immoralities, and lies. Instead, she just grinned as if she were unaware she had just been humiliated and made to look like a helpless female. She avoided calling him Criminal Trump or Cheating Trump or Comrade Trump. Democrats have to stop behaving like scared little chickens and tell it like it is. Hillary had a weak voice and lacked the personal appeal of Reagan and Obama. This was the real reason for her loss.

Although Hillary has exceptional experience, knowledge, and accomplishments, she did not show a fighter's instinct to fearlessly attack her opponent. People want a leader who is bold, aggressive, and courageous. If the Democrats do not learn the lessons that Trump gave them, they will not win many elections.

A stronger, more likable candidate would have defeated Trump. Trump won because Democrats put up a weak personality, because the presidential election is not based on the popular-vote count, and because the Republican's dishonest campaign of hate and fear was effective among gullible voters.

It has also been established by all the security and law enforcement agencies that Russia was extensively involved in social media distortions and lies attacking Hillary. The amount of damage caused by the Russian advertising campaign is not known, but those ads must have some effects or campaigns would not be spending millions on TV ads and social media ads.

In spite of the fact that Trump has demonstrated the morals, and irresponsibility of a drug dealer with the maturity of a Valley Girl, he is audacious, outrageous, and confident, which are the things people want in a leader. Hillary was the opposite. Hillary famously said, "When they go low, we go high." People don't care about high and low. Voters want a hero who would boldly lead the charge into battle with both guns blazing. Hillary was right when she admitted, "I'm not a politician."

Negative campaigns work. Republican campaigns are nearly all negative and always based on distorted and incomplete versions of the facts. The Republican policy of constant character assassination of Democrats regardless of the truth has been a roaring success. The individual issues are not important. The only thing that matters is creating a negative public perception of Democrats. Once people have been convinced that Democrats are the enemy, they will believe the most ridiculous nonsense imaginable. Some people believe the incredible lie that the Ku Klux Klan was a gang of liberals. Manipulating public perceptions of reality is the gold prize of politics. Republicans have managed to get a lot of people to believe the ridiculous nonsense that Democrats are communists who want to destroy democracy and freedom.

When you achieve such powerful Jedi mind control, you can get away with anything no matter how illegal, immoral, or illogical as Trump has done. Trump can tell his zealous zombies that Democrats are Klingons from outer space, and they would believe it.

Democrats need to hammer loud, clear, and often about all the lies, scandals, failures, hypocrisy, and deceit of the Republicans. Democrats don't even have to make up 10,000 lies the way Trump has[65]. The truth of recent Republican failures, dishonesty, and pandering to billionaires is more than enough to expose the Republicans' disregard for the working class. Democrats should have exposed the truth of the slanderous Republican lies about Benghazi, about the Clinton Foundation, and about everything else.

Democrats will have to show that they have the courage, confidence, and credibility to go on the offensive and directly expose all the Republican disinformation. Democrats should confront Republicans face-to-face with specific, pointed questions that expose Republican actions that are never in the voter's best interests.

A few examples are as follows:

- Why did Republicans repeal the fairness in broadcasting regulations?
- Why did Republicans repeal net neutrality (free internet)?
- Why did Republicans vote to prohibit free-market negotiations of drug prices?
- Why did Republicans vote against the background checks that everyone wants?
- Why are Republicans opposed to consumer financial protections?
- Why do Republicans refuse to do anything about the thousands of gun deaths?

Republicans have a track record of avoiding incriminating questions. When faced with questions like these, they always go off on some other subject and refuse to give simple, direct answers. Even when an interviewer repeats the question several times, the Republican will refuse to answer the question. Eventually the interviewer gives up, but the point is made that the Republican cannot give an honest answer.

Americans, including Republicans, disapprove of the kidnapping of immigrant children, disapprove of the welfare-for-billionaires tax cuts, and disapprove of ignoring global warming. Yet it seems Democrats rarely raise these issues. Many Republican politicians do not agree with Trump but are afraid to stand up for their beliefs because they do not want to alienate Trump voters.

Democrats are always playing defense, while Republicans are always on the offense. Defense does not win elections. Until Democrats adapt aggressive offensive strategies and tactics, they will always be fighting with one hand tied behind their backs and will struggle to win elections. Republicans are experts at manipulating public opinion but terrible at governing, at economics, and at foreign relations.

It is not clear why Republican politicians have a lot of trouble operating within the law. Table 9 shows that during the past 55 years, Republican administrations had a lot more criminal indictments and convictions than Democrat administrations had. In fact, they are not even close. Republican had over 147 indictments and 94 convictions. Democrats had only three indictments and one conviction. Although there is no proof, it appears as if Republicans indeed do have a much different attitude toward government and laws. It seems as if they consider government as a means to an end and not an end in itself. And they always put party ahead of country.

Table 9
Criminal Activity by Party

EXECUTIVE BRANCH CRIMINAL ACTIVITIES

	Criminal Indictments	Criminal Convictions	Prison Sentences
DEMOCRATS			
Obama	0	0	0
Clinton	2	1	1
Carter	1	0	0
Johnson	0	0	0
TOTAL	3	1	1
REPUBLICANS			
Trump	27+	5+	?
Bush 2	16	16	9
Bush 1	1	1	1
Reagan	26	16	8
Ford	1	1	1
Nixon	76	55	15
TOTAL	147	94	34

Personalities

Democrats need candidates who are aggressive and go after Republicans like a pit bull on LSD. It would be refreshing to see a Democrat break out of the traditional mold of politely and respectfully disagreeing with his or her opponent. You do not get points for good manners. The type of candidate needed is a brilliant, no-holds-barred trial lawyer who can decisively drive a stake into the heart of his opponent's statements. This requires an expansive memory with instant recall and a command of powerful, emotional words. But the rhetoric must focus on the opponent and never against any of his supporters. Obama was able to recover from a mistake of this type, while Hillary was not.

Many Democrats seem to suffer from severe paucity of passion. They talk to an audience of hardworking motorcycle mechanics and firefighters as if they were presenting a PhD thesis to a panel of Caltech astrophysicists. Audience members keep turning to one another saying, "Tell me when to applaud because I don't know what he's talking about."

Democrats cannot afford to ignore one of the basic laws of elections—the candidate with the most charismatic credibility usually wins. This type of person shows confidence, ability, and trustworthiness. Voters are drawn to this type of candidate. They feel he is always telling it like it is and is sincerely concerned about their well-being. In 2016, neither candidate fit this profile, so there was a low turnout of voters. Ronald Reagan, Jack Kennedy, Barack Obama, and Bill Clinton had this type of personality. Voters were drawn to them because they gave the impression that they were honest, competent and sincerely concerned about the voter. In 2019, the early candidates that best fit this profile are Elisabeth Warren and Joe Biden. But other candidates might also fit this profile.

Opinions vs. Facts

It seems illogical, but no amount of facts, logic, or even common sense reasoning can get some people to change their minds. Strong opinions cannot be altered even with all the facts and logic in the world. It has been said that "you can't win an argument with facts."

When people embrace feelings and opinions, they automatically reject anything that erodes their commitment to those opinions regardless of the contrary evidence. Their attitude is "I'll see it when I believe it." Psychologists call this cognitive dissonance [66]. If someone believes Trump's lies, mountains of DNA, fingerprints, confessions, photographs, witnesses, and videos proving the opposite will not get them to change their opinion. They become totally impervious to facts, logic, and common sense. They are so completely indoctrinated that from their point of view, the real world of verified, substantiated, proven facts are considered fake news.

When Trump was caught talking about his celebrity license to molest women without retribution, his followers dismissed it as nothing to be concerned about. Had a Democrat said the same thing, Republicans would be rioting in the streets for weeks. The opinions of Republicans are rarely affected by real-world events.

Although thoroughly proven to be false, many Republicans continue to believe all the lies about illegal voters, Benghazi, the Uranium One deal, the Clinton Foundation, Obama's birthplace, and the Iran nuclear agreement. Even though these lies have all been thoroughly debunked many times, Republicans cannot separate their emotional commitment to the distortions of reality. This is the overriding principle behind Republican manipulation of public opinion. Democrats should clearly expose all the lies and hypocrisy of their opponents and then keep repeating them over and over.

As noted previously, Fox News viewers are less informed than viewers of other media and 68% of its contents are opinions, not facts. The objective of the far-right media is to cultivate a false image of Democrats. Trump's frequent tactic is to create an alternate reality where everything is a disaster and only he can fix it. Trump charges that everything is broken, everyone is incompetent, everyone is dishonest, and absolutely everything accomplished under Obama is a total catastrophe. He makes these false accusations with such conviction and confidence that gullible people actually believe all of it and nothing will ever change their minds.

Table 10
Strange Things Republicans Continue to Believe

	A SAMPLE OF LIES THAT MANY REPUBLICANS BELIEVE
54%	Believe Obama is a Muslim
17%	See more people in Trump inauguration photo than in Obama's
46%	Believe Hillary is involved in child sex in a Pizza restaurant
45%	Believe Obama Care has "death panels"
48%	Believe 5 million illegal aliens voted in 2016
75%	Believe CO_2 emissions do not increease global warmiing
66%	Believe Muslims are implementing Sharia Law in America
57%	Believe humans did not evolve over billions of years

Table 10 is a partial list of the incredible nonsense that many Republicans believe. Instead of dismissing these tactics as impossible for voters to believe, Democrats should be waging an all-out war on the slander and distortions of facts that are the basis of Republican campaigns [67].

Voter Fraud

In the past, Americans lost trust and confidence in a candidate when they learned how they were deceived by lies. However, today, honesty is no longer considered a requirement for a candidate. Consider Trump's lie that five million illegal immigrants voted against him. Trump groupies actually believe this nonsense. This is just one of the thousands of lies Trump has made. Here is a review of this one big lie.

Trump wants the public to believe millions of illegals voted for Hillary. He needs people to believe this lie so he can claim he won the popular vote, which he did not win. Also, it is part of the constant strategy of getting people to believe they are the victims of a liberal voting conspiracy.

A review of the numbers shows how this is impossible. Several organizations have studied the number of illegal aliens in the USA. Some have estimated it could be as high as 20 million. A conservative estimate of the percentage that are of voting age and capable of voting is 60%. A conservative estimate of the percentage that can understand English is 50% If 5 million illegal aliens voted in 2016, this would be 83% of 6 million who are old enough to vote and understand English. Such a high percentage of illegals voting is just not possible. The percentage of Americans who voted was only 55%. An undocumented construction foreman said, "We never voted in our home country. We have no interest in politics. And we don't understand the speeches."

Like most hardworking people, their thoughts and concerns are about finding work, about feeding their families, about the MLS soccer scores, about assimilating their kids and themselves into the community, and about avoiding deportation. Few of them know who the governor is or who the vice president of the USA is. On Election Day, they make sure they do not accidentally wander anywhere close to a polling place.

Yet Republicans expect us to believe that on Election Day, millions of these illegals suddenly understood English, became interested in politics, lost all fear of deportation, and boldly walked into government-run election-polling places. If you believe that, I got some magic beans to sell you.

Trump and Republicans want you to believe illegal aliens are voting at a higher rate than Americans and none of them voted for Trump. This is a good example of how Republicans use lies to build fear of immigrants to manipulate naive voters.

Unfortunately, there are many people on the right who, over the years, have been conditioned to believe stuff like this. The tactic is successful because it gets a lot of gullible people outraged at illegal immigrants.

On May 11, 2017, Trump signed an executive order creating the Presidential Advisory Commission on Election Integrity. This commission was directed to identify all the illegals who had voted. The commission knew this was a big waste of time, so they spent a few nights convening at the Georgetown Gentlemen's entertainment club and then had an intern write a report that said they could not find any evidence of illegal voters. Trump does not release reports or any information that contradicts his public statements. So this report was buried.

However, this did not dissuade the Fox News audience from continuing to believe it was "all those illegal Mexicans" who were undermining our elections and the Russian Main Intelligence Directorate (GRU) had nothing to do with the election.

In 2008 Republicans told us that Obama won only because many people on welfare voted for him. This too was dishonest because, like illegals, welfare recipients have no interest in elections and are not registered to vote.

Even though the lies about illegal voters have been thoroughly exposed and debunked, Republican voters continue to believe the lies. No amount of data, logic, or common sense could ever get Fox viewers to believe the facts. They just shout "fake news" and continue to believe whatever nonsense they are instructed to believe. (See the "Seventh Law of Politics"—Republicans continue repeating the lies long after they have been debunked.)

Voting Problems

A major threat to America and democracy and freedom is all the people who don't vote. Fewer Democrats voted in the 2016 general election compared to the primary elections. America cannot afford to have repeats of the past Republican disasters of the Iraq war of 2003, the Great Republican Recession of 2008, the mass murders of dozens of little schoolchildren, the billionaire tax loopholes of 2018, the rejection of the global warming, the resumption of the Iran nuclear-bomb program, and now the expansion of the North Korean nuclear-bomb program. If we want to avoid these national catastrophes, we must get people to vote.

In Australia, everyone is required to vote or else they pay a fine of $170. Republicans would fiercely fight against a similar law in the United States. However, it might be possible to get Americans to vote by exchanging their voting receipts for free lottery tickets. It is illegal for political parties to campaign at polling locations, but handing out lottery tickets to everyone who voted should be legal, at least until Republicans passed laws prohibiting it.

In addition to all the citizens who do not vote, Republicans in many states have passed various voter-suppression laws. These laws are intended to discourage or prohibit people who may vote for a democrat from voting. The voting registration laws in North Dakota and Wisconsin have strict voter-ID laws that require correct details like current addresses and form of the voter's name. This is a problem for Native Americans who live on reservations and for minorities in general. Georgia has refused to process tens of thousands of voter registrations in 2018 [68]. Florida illegally purged thousands of names from their registration databases. Several states have removed hundreds of voting locations in black and Hispanic areas to reduce the number of Democrat voters [69]. Extreme gerrymandering of congressional districts has been employed in many states. Gerrymandering is a scheme to define congressional districts in a way to spread non-Republican voters across areas that are solidly Republican to ensure Republicans win those districts.

Partisan gerrymandering cannot be done in California because the geographical outlines of congressional districts has been turned over to an independent, nonpartisan committee. This should be done in all states. However, Republican states would not accept any process that does not give them an advantage in elections.

Conservative Disinformation Campaigns

Republicans understand how to manipulate public perceptions. They know that most people are concerned with only one or two issues. They know they can attack their opponents with greatly distorted versions of the facts and never be held accountable for misleading the public. They did not enjoy this license before the repeal of the fairness in broadcasting regulations in 1987. Here are a few examples of false propaganda that voters should be familiar with.

Uranium One—Republican Party operatives knew Hillary Clinton had little involvement with the sale of Uranium One to Russia, but their primary objective was to always accuse Hillary of misconduct regardless of the facts. The constant twisting and spinning of everything regarding Democrats is the lifeblood of Republicans. Many Republicans still believe the lies that Hillary Clinton sold uranium to Russia even though it has been proven to be completely false. The far-right media conveniently omits the fact that the all-nuclear sales require the approval of nine agencies and government departments:

- Secretary of the Treasury
- Attorney General
- Secretary of Defense
- State Department
- Commerce and Energy
- Nuclear Regulatory Commission
- United States Trade Representative
- Homeland Security
- Office of Science and Technology Policy

Hillary approved only what all the agencies had already approved. But these facts were irrelevant to Hillary's political opponents. They continued to accuse Hillary of selling Uranium One to Russia. People continued to believe these lies long after they had been debunked.

Republicans falsely accused the Clinton Foundation of corruption and of being a front to funnel bribes to Hillary Clinton. These were just more Republican lies because charity-rating agencies have always rated the Clinton Foundation as one of the best charities [70]. It has the top rating, and 87% of its income went to charity programs. The Clinton Foundation is highly efficient at using donations for charitable projects all over the world and in the USA. It did not funnel donations to the Clintons. Despite the facts, many people continued to believe the Republican lies about the Clintons and the Clinton Foundation. Meanwhile, the Trump Foundation was forced to shut down because Trump was caught using the foundation as a tax-free expense account[71].

The Benghazi affair was another example of Republican tactic to constantly spread misinformation and lies about Democrats. Seven nonpartisan military, CIA, and congressional investigations including a Republican investigation found that Hillary had done nothing wrong regarding the Benghazi attack[72]. Regardless of all these investigations, Republicans continued to blame Hillary for somehow being responsible for the attack on the US consulate in Benghazi that killed four Americans. They accomplished this by never letting the issue die, and they were aided by Democrats who refused to expose these Republican lies as a major issue.

Small Government

Republicans claim smaller government is better government. But Republicans have done the opposite. They have drastically increased the national debt and have policies that control our personal lives.

They demand government control women's bodies and health. They demand government control on whom you can love and marry. They demand government control what you can and cannot smoke. They demand those engaged in victimless activities be treated the same as dangerous criminals. They want government control over what religions can be practiced.

Republicans claim to want fiscally responsible budgets and spending, yet Republican presidents have always increased the national debt that is now approaching the astronomical level of $20 trillion[73]. Republicans also claim to be opposed to all welfare programs, but once in office, they forget about welfare spending and instead concentrate their efforts on spending more of your tax dollars on the military that already is the largest in the galaxy and has hundreds of unnecessary bases all over the world. Republicans cheerfully spend billions on more million-dollar stealth fighters, on more nuclear submarines, and even on a space force that presumably will protect us from a Klingon invasion.

When Obama was president Tea Party Republicans were adamant about reducing the national debt. But Trump's enormous increases are acceptable to the Tea Party Republicans. In other words "small government" applies only to Democrats.

Trump

UN members laughed at Trump during his UN speech. Across 37 countries, the confidence in the US presidency has dropped from 64% for Obama to merely 22% for Trump [74]. Even though Trump is recognized around the world as a pathological, compulsive liar, his fans either believe all his lies or claim they do not matter. However, if a Democrat were that dishonest, Republicans would be marching all over America with torches and pitchforks chanting "Lock him up."

Trump and his Republican accomplices have left a trail of mistakes, dishonesty, and failures, which include everything from international agreements to tax breaks for billionaires to clear violations of the Constitution, such as the emoluments clause.

For example, although 83% of voters opposed the repeal of Obama's net neutrality rules (free and equal internet service for everyone), Trump went ahead and repealed net neutrality anyway so corporations could charge you to use the internet. [75] (See the "Fifth Law of Politics"—Republicans always put interests of the superwealthy ahead of the working class).

California government is concerned more about consumers than about corporations. So California ignored Trump and passed its own net neutrality laws.

Trump is committed to repealing everything Obama did because he hates Obama. Democrats are such poor politicians they did not bother to make this a major scandal the way Republicans did with their twisting and spinning of everything regarding Hillary Clinton.

Trump's claim that Obama was not born in the United States has been discredited several times in various ways, including an original birth certificate. Even Trump himself no longer denies Obama was born in America. Yet 57% of Trump voters continue to believe the lie that Obama was not born in the USA. These political attacks by Republicans are totally fact-free fiction. Trump, without the slightest evidence, insisted Obama had ordered the wiretapping of his offices. Almost immediately, this was proven to be just another of Trump's many lies. Yet people continued to believe these lies long after they had been exposed as false. (See the "Seventh Law of Politics"—Republicans continue repeating all their debunked lies.)

Trump flat-out lied when he claimed no one at all in his campaign had any contact with any Russians. Then the truth came out about the Russian meetings, but Trump never admitted his lies and instead just blamed the media for reporting "fake news."

The Moscow Project reported :

> A total of 251 contacts between Trump's team and Russia-linked operatives have been identified, including at least 37 meetings.

Even after Trump's lies had been exposed, his league of lemmings obediently chanted "Nobel, Nobel" as soon as the secret crowd plants started the mantra.

Good, religious, family-values people just looked the other way when all of Trump's cheating with prostitutes and extramarital affairs during his three marriages were brought up. They were not bothered by all his dishonesty. What happened to all those family values that Republicans claim only they have?

Trump also lied when he said New York Muslims cheered the 9/11 attacks and that his inauguration had the largest attendance in history and that Russia did nothing to affect the 2016 election. It did not bother Trump when he was questioned about all his lies. He just changed the subject and attacked the nonpartisan media. He continued on and never bothered to explain his lies [65].

Trump's press secretary, Sarah Sanders, also brushed aside questions about his lies without providing any answers. In an interview with Chuck Todd, Trump spokesperson Kellyanne Conway provided a windfall of material to the nation's comedians when she justified Sean Spicer's outright lies by claiming Spicer was "giving alternative facts." Todd was stunned and had to muffle his laughter before saying, "Alternative facts are *not* facts. They're lies." Kellyanne refused to address Todd's question and instead changed the subject as she always does when she is asked hardball questions. Echoing Sarah Palin, Kellyanne chided Todd for not asking the questions she wanted him to ask her[76]. It seems Kellyanne thinks an interview is a discussion where she first gives the answers and then the interviewer provides the questions as in the Johnny Carson "Carnac the Magnificent" comedy routine[77].

It seems many people automatically accept whatever falsehoods they are given attacking Democrats. They do not bother to even consider whether or not the attacks make any sense. This helps explain why Republicans do not want critical thinking taught in schools. This was actually stated in a campaign platform.

Republican Campaign Statement

> Knowledge-Based Education—We oppose the teaching of Higher Order Thinking Skills (HOTS) (values clarification), critical thinking skills and similar programs that are simply a relabeling of Outcome-Based Education (OBE) (mastery learning) which focus on behavior modification and have the purpose of challenging the student's fixed beliefs and undermining parental authority [78, 79].

Just like defense lawyers in court do not want intelligent, critical-thinking jurors carefully analyzing their defense arguments, Republicans also do not want smart voters picking apart their dishonest attacks on Democrats.

The objective of all these false Republican accusations is not to persuade voters that specific illicit actions have been committed but rather to manipulate the public into thinking Democrats have different values from the typical American. And they will continue to fabricate false charges against Democrats because many voters readily believe all the lies. Trial lawyers have a saying regarding courtroom lies, "You can't un-ring a bell after it has rung." It is the same with all the Republican lies. They never go away. This persistence of Republican lies even after being fully exposed was ridiculed by Bill Maher and labeled zombie lies because they never die [80]. (See the "Seventh Law of Politics"—Republicans continue repeating their lies long after they have been debunked.)

This begs the question "Why are Trump and Republicans such prolific liars?" Sure, all politicians can be loose with the facts, but today's Republicans are far beyond the norm. Their dishonest attacks on Democrats are extremely misleading and never contain the complete and accurate facts. They were not able to do this before Reagan got the fairness in broadcasting law repealed. If Democrats ever get a filibuster proof majority, reinstating the media fairness rules should be top priority and would include cable and satellite transmissions along with TV and radio.

The reason Republicans constantly lie about Democrats, even when no elections are imminent, is that if they were honest, they would not win elections. The typical voter is not familiar with all the complexities of government and foreign affairs, so they believe all Trump's lies about health care, about the economy, about Obama, about military budgets, about Mexicans, and about everything else. Republicans are forced to lie so they can win elections. They know they cannot win elections unless they constantly repeat misleading information about their opponents and about their true goals.

PART SIX

Beyond the Horizon

If overpopulation is not controlled voluntarily, it will be controlled involuntarily by increases in diseases, starvation, and wars.
—Prince Philip

The USA and the world are in historical transition phases. We have an exploding human population, we have severe shortages of freshwater, we have a rapidly changing global climate, automation is eliminating the need for unskilled workers, and we have the greatest political divide in history. The world cannot continue on this trajectory.

When people all over the world are starving while living next to lavish penthouses with golden flowerpots, indoor tennis courts, and an army of minimum-wage staff, the general population has nothing to lose and everything to gain through rebellions and wars. We are not at that point yet, but it is looming over the horizon.

The most serious problem the world has today is not Muslim terrorists or another Hitler-type dictator. The most serious problem is world population. Many problems are a consequence of population explosion. Furthermore, we are exacerbating the problems with our policies and progress. The world population has increased by a factor of four from 2 billion to nearly 8 billion in less than 100 years. If this continues, the world could become a real-life version of a postapocalyptic Hollywood movie.

Automation

The automation of countless manual activities has exploded over the past few decades. At first it was just self-service gas pumps, but soon, there were bank tellers and checkout clerks at grocery stores and even at Home Depot. Out of public sight, virtually all production and shipping jobs have been automated. Megamachines are employed in coal mines and iron mines. Not long ago, the loading and unloading of transport ships required teams of longshoremen. Most of these dockworkers have been replaced with automation. Las Vegas casinos are using automated blackjack dealers displayed on a big video screen and employing digital cards instead of the usual decks of cards.

In the near future, cars will run without drivers the same way nearly all elevators now run without operators. (That's right. Elevators used to have operators.) The traveler tells the computer in the driverless car the destination and is automatically taken there. Since human error causes most accidents, the elimination of human involvement will greatly reduce accidents. The ripple effect creates a great reduction in insurance companies and body shops. The shift to electric cars, which have few moving parts, will eliminate most auto-repair jobs. Gas stations and fuel companies will disappear.

Bus drivers, truck drivers, and pilots will be replaced by automation. Even a backup pilot is not needed because a plane can be controlled from the ground. Cargo planes would be the first to try this. This is a routine operation for our military drones. Schools continue to increase the number of online classes. The number of well-paid skilled employees is slowly being reduced by not replacing employees lost through normal attrition.

Entire industries have been eliminated or greatly reduced by our smartphones. We no longer have hard-copy encyclopedias, *Yellow Pages*, and dictionaries. City map books, pocket cameras, and calculators are nearly extinct. Newspapers, books, and record albums are disappearing. Home telephones, calendars, and taxi services are no longer ubiquitous. Those services provided jobs for millions of families. Smartphone apps have created some jobs but not nearly as many that are lost. The new gig economy has also created some jobs, but the pay is minimal. Uber drivers in New York and San Francisco have a higher net income than taxi drivers. But in smaller cities, Uber drivers make less than taxi drivers do[81].

So what will happen to all these displaced workers? Some will be employed in emerging industries, but probably not all of them. Meanwhile, the reductions in operational labor costs are not passed on to the consumer but instead go toward increased corporate profits and to astronomical CEO salaries, thereby increasing the already-enormous income gap between the top 1% and everyone else. Also big corporations are loaded with cash that in the past went to consumers and employees. Apple is sitting on $300 billion cash, which is larger than the GDP and annual budgets of most countries. There is no need for the billions of dollars Trump gave to corporations and billionaires with his excessive corporate welfare tax policies. Trump paid for these unnecessary corporate handouts by increasing the national debt. This means the money going to the superwealthy will be paid by you and the other American taxpayers. Of course Trump and his family do not have to worry about this because they do not pay taxes. Trump paid no federal taxes from 1985 to 1994.

Population Policies

While we are reducing the number of human jobs, we are also making breakthroughs in medical research that is extending the life expectancy of everyone that has access to health care. The ability to manipulate and customize DNA is perhaps the greatest accomplishment of science—even greater than space travel. Indications are within the lives of people living today; we will have cures for cancer, Alzheimer's, and many other diseases. It is very possible that life expectancy will continue its upward trend. In wealthy communities, it could even accelerate. Our great-grandchildren could live for 130 years. This would accelerate the increase of the world population and all the problems that entails. Normal retirement age will have to be increased to at least 80 or 85 years old. But that takes jobs away from the new, young workers.

Social conservatives continue working to eliminate all abortions, including those only a few days along. This also increases the population and comes with unintended consequences affecting all of us.

In their book *Freakonomics*, Levitt and Dubner explain how the legalization of abortions in 1973 led to a pronounced drop in crime and in welfare rolls about 15 years later. So if President Trump is successful in imposing peculiar religious beliefs on the nation, we can expect serious, unintended side effects of increases in crime and welfare recipients.

Raising cattle for the billions of hamburgers consumed each day is a large contributor to global warming. Cattle burping produces large quantities of methane, a greenhouse gas.

If we do not solve these problems of unskilled unemployment, global warming, droughts, extreme divisiveness, overpopulation, and extreme income inequality, it is possible that general living conditions could become intolerable, similar to those of the fourteenth century when about one of every three people died in a matter of hours after contracting the Black Death.

Desperate people resort to desperate measures. We could be faced with great wars like nothing of the past. We could be fighting over resources with nuclear weapons and unstoppable germ warfare. Entire countries and populations could be destroyed in a matter of days or weeks.

This can be avoided if all countries and all peoples recognize the problems before it is too late and start working together to solve them. Unfortunately, humans do not have a good record of cooperation. Social conservatives always resist changes necessary to mitigate these problems. Today, we have large numbers of conservatives who refuse to accept the possibilities of serious problems caused by enormous wealth inequality, by global warming, by overpopulation, by automation, and by permanent droughts. This can change with educational programs, but it is difficult to educate people who are emotionally committed to their religious or political beliefs. They reject everything that does not confirm their misinformed opinions.

This refusal to even consider new information that threatens entrenched beliefs could be the black bullet that ends the current epoch of humanity. Intelligent, sensible, proactive leadership is critical to surviving these encroaching disasters. However, we have recently learned that competent leadership cannot be taken for granted as it was in the past.

Chart 11
World Population History

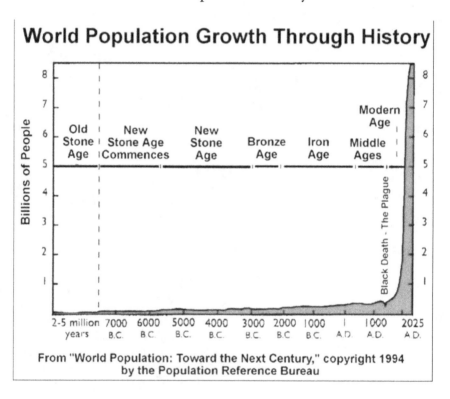

Chart 12
Life Expectancy

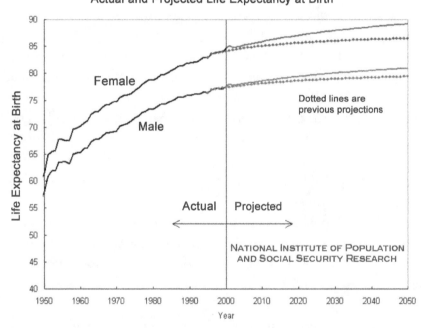

Source: National Institute of Population and Social Security Research[82]

Permanent Political Divide

Some of the major issues driving the enormous political divide have been highlighted here. Political allegiance has replaced religion as the basis for self-identity and distrust of all outsiders. We select associates based on their political views more than on their religion or social status. Likewise, we shun those with opposing views as if they were space aliens. The political divide in the US is greater and more intense than at any time since 1865. It is not unusual for family members and lifelong friends to suddenly become completely alienated from one another because of political differences.

American politics have become brutally uncivilized. It is as if we are two separate countries reluctantly sharing a single government that neither country completely accepts. This great divide can be resolved if the major parties are able to work together with cooperation and compromise. In the past, presidents played golf with the leaders of the opposite party. For the past several years, they do not even talk to one another.

When Obama was elected, Republicans pledged to never vote for anything proposed by Democrats regardless of the pros and cons or the needs of the country.

In 2009, Republicans filibustered all of Obama's economic recovery and job bills and then blamed Democrats for a slow recovery from the Republican recession of 2008. Any politician who lets his citizens suffer bankruptcies and job loses strictly for selfish partisan reasons is the worst kind of politician.

Republican John Boehner said, "We're going to do everything—and I mean everything we can do—to kill it, stop it, slow it down, whatever we can"[83]. That is not government. That is a childish temper tantrum.

No presidential candidate ever promised to put his opponent in jail. But Republican Trump did exactly that even though he never had any evidence of a crime. No political party would have accepted another country sabotaging our national election. But on July 26, 2016, Trump publicly invited Russia to perform illegal election hacking: "Russia, if you're listening, I hope you're able to find the 30,000 emails that are missing." This unbelievable encouragement of illegal foreign sabotage shocked the nation. No other president would ever invite a hostile nation to hack into our government computers, but Donald Trump did it openly on television. This is one more example of putting party above country.

With the election of Trump, many felt they no longer had to cover up their racist beliefs. One California bed-and-breakfast owner turned away an Asian couple with reservations telling them, "I don't have to rent to you now because Trump is president." Many such encounters of racism have been reported, and they were justified by the belief that Trump had legitimatized racism. Hate crimes jumped 17% soon after Trump was elected. [84]

How did the US become so severely divided in the past few decades? Repeal of fairness in media was a big part of it. But it must also be because of either genetics or life experiences. The field of genopolitical research has recently emerged. This involves genetic studies to identify correlations between political beliefs and DNA.

It has been found that there is a strong correlation between the DRD4 gene and political opinions [85]. Studies have shown that 40% of our political views have a genetic component. However, an individual's social environment also has a strong effect. An individual's political persuasion is not totally deterministic, but there is a statistical correlation to genes and environment. This helps explain why we have red states and blue states. This also helps explain why some people are impervious to facts and figures and why they cling to their fact-free opinions.

Social Networks

Dr. Solomon Asch conducted conformity studies in 1951 at Swarthmore College in Pennsylvania. The goal was to determine to what extent people would change their beliefs to fit into the group. Subjects were given three choices—two obviously wrong and one correct. In the control trial, all subjects picked the correct answer. They announced their answers verbally one at a time.

In subsequent trials, all subjects except one were secretly directed to pick the wrong answer. The subject who was last in line received no instructions. 37% of the time the last subject in line announced that he picked the same wrong answer as all those before him. The experiment was repeated many times in different ways with different people.

The conclusion is that about 37% of the time, people will believe whatever others tell them rather than their own eyes and ears. This helps explain why we have red states and blue states. People are heavily influenced by those they are in contact with or who are part of their social network [86].

A Divided Country

In part 2, it was shown how society and government gradually but permanently changed after printing and literacy was expanded to all citizens. When the masses learned about abuses by the church and by the monarchies, revolutions spread throughout the literate world. In the recent past, we have seen a significant drop-off in newspaper circulations, in bookstores, and even in novels. It seems reading is now limited primarily to pop culture and legal documents. Also during this same period, the fairness in broadcasting law was repealed; and immediately, extreme, one-sided, biased conservative media sprung up. It is not a coincidence that during the same period the political landscape became sharply divided. A large portion of the population no longer got information from impartial traditional sources but only from politically biased media. The conservative media did not adhere to the long-established policies of good reporting such as multiple sources to confirm a story, printing corrections when errors are discovered, and covering all sides of a story without bias.

The net results of the influence of social pressures, the decline in reading, and the biased media channels is an electorate that is heavily bifurcated with little middle ground. A significant portion of the population has no interest in political issues and would never read a book such as this one. Information TV shows do not interest them. They find watching Jerry Springer and reruns of *I Love Lucy* more interesting than

Meet the Press. This lack of interest in government creates an electorate that is naive and easily influenced by misinformation and one-sided reporting.

There is no disagreement that the USA has never been so polarized since the Civil War. Depending on which party is in office, a large portion of the country is forced to live under policies and regulations they are strongly opposed to. The rest of the country gets to dictate laws, taxes, and programs that affect everyone, whether or not they like them.

It is nearly impossible to properly run a country when the citizens are so sharply divided. It is not a secret that Trump has always hated Obama and has been determined to reverse absolutely everything accomplished by Obama. It does not matter that a majority of citizens object to reversing Obama's accomplishments.

Another Civil War is unlikely, but we have already had several armed conflicts between government forces and citizen groups that disagreed with democratically established policies.

After Obama was reelected in 2012, a Texas poll showed that half of the Texas Republicans favored Texas secession [87]. After Trump was elected in 2016, polls showed that between one-fourth and one-third of Californians favored secession [88]. Also a significant number of people in states other than Texas and California were in favor of getting rid of those two states.

Despite the great political differences, Americans are not ready to break up the 50 states. However, it is possible to retain the union and still separate the states in a win-win solution.

The United Alliance

The problem is that all states are required to live under a single Constitution. If conservatives and liberals had different constitutions, everyone would be happy and family gatherings would be as joyful as they used to be. The Europeans formed the European Union by combining several countries under one umbrella organization. The US could accomplish the same thing in reverse by separating groups of states into semiautonomous regions. The 50 states, could be combined into groups of states with similar political ideologies.

This could be called the American Union or the United Alliance (UA). The regions would all share a single military and resolve interregional conflicts with a Supreme Court as it is done today. But internal issues would be resolved locally without affecting the other regions. One region could outlaw all abortions and same-sex marriages without affecting any of the other regions. Conservatives that want big corporations spending unlimited amounts on elections could continue to operate under the controversial Citizens United decision. [89] A region could also establish the Bible-based government that they have been demanding. Regions could even restrict voting to certain races and ethnicities. It would be a win-win for everyone.

There would be completely tariff-free trade between these UA regions. Each region would have its own president and constitution and could create a truly democratic process instead of the quasi-democratic process we now have.

Each region would have senators in the umbrella UA government proportional to its population. These senators would select a president or a director from their ranks. Each region would keep it's own taxes. This would not have the problem we now have with some "giver" states, like California, supporting "taker" states, like South Carolina. This UA umbrella government would be concerned with only high-level issues that involve all regions the same as done in the European Union.

The liberal and conservative regions would no longer be fighting with each other, and yet everyone would still live in America. It could take years to get all the details worked out, but in the end, everyone would have the kind of government that they deserve.

There is a second alternative to the divided-country problem, and it worked in the past. There was much more cooperation and compromise in the US government before Reagan repealed the fairness in broadcasting law. The fairness law required political radio and TV to present both sides of every issue and argument. Republicans have always opposed fairness in broadcasting. This is why Reagan repealed the law.

It is clear that those who listen to Fox News, Alex Jones, and all the other one-sided political media outlets have a very different image of politics and parties than those who do not listen to these strongly biased channels. There cannot be two different versions of the truth and the facts. So requiring broadcast programs to present both sides of issues is the fair and proper thing to do. People are free to believe one side or the other, but they can only do this if they have complete and accurate information of both sides. Unfortunately, that is not what Republicans want.

Republicans oppose restoring the fairness in broadcasting law. Republicans are still opposed to fairness as they always have been since it was first passed in 1949, so restoring fairness would never happen unless Democrats could override Republican obstruction to fairness in media.

EPILOGUE

The overriding message of this book is that social conservatives have always been on the wrong side of history. Conservatives have always opposed changes to the status quo. However, after a generation or two, conservatives have accepted the progressive accomplishments of social liberals. Today, social conservatives no longer oppose the abolition of slavery, female voting, labor rights, cannabis consumption, same-sex marriages, general health-care availability, or any of the many other freedoms and rights conservatives have opposed in the past. Social liberals have been behind all social progress of the past 300 years, and yet many Americans are unaware of who and what social liberals really are.

History has shown over and over that today's Republicans are experts at manipulating public opinion by cultivating extreme hatred and fear through distortions, deceit, and lies. But their record at governing has been disastrous, involving avoidable recessions and wars. The economy has always done better under the Democrats.

Democrats need to understand that playing defense does not inspire voters. Democrats must find charismatic leaders who have strong personalities and inspire trust and confidence. Democrats also need to fight back loud and often against all the disinformation and false personal attacks of the Republican distortion machine.

Although America and the world face challenges that humanity has never confronted in the past, there is hope of mitigating these problems. But it will require intelligent and cooperative leadership. Ignoring the impending problems is the worst thing we can do.

Continuation of extreme political discord and divisiveness prevents America from achieving the stability and progress it is capable of. Restoring the fairness in media regulations would be a good start to address that obstacle. A more drastic solution would be to let the red regions and the blue regions adopt their own independent constitutions but remain within the United Alliance. This has the benefit of everyone getting the government that they deserve.

Conservative Republicans have been relentless for decades in carrying out the dictates of the superwealthy by opposing affordable health care, by eliminating limits on reckless speculations, by suppressing living wages, and with enormous tax breaks for millionaires. Conservatives have been relentless in suppressing gender equality, spreading hate, suppressing voting and democracy, and eliminating personal freedoms.

Remember, freedom is not free. You cannot stand idly by while Republicans continue to destroy our freedoms, our prosperity, and our lives. You must do whatever you can to stop the conservative plans to take the US back to the days of superrich and superpoor that existed before the great liberal movements and revolutions of the past. You must spread the truth to everyone. You must become active in election campaigns. You cannot roll over and surrender to the enemies of the working class. You must stand up for your rights or suffer the consequences.

Your future is in your hands; do not drop it. Do something.

APPENDIX

Everything You Need to Know

1. The fairness in broadcasting law was passed in 1949 to prohibit broadcasting one-sided false propaganda. It required that both sides have equal time.
2. Republicans repealed this law over strong objections by Democrats. This tells you everything you need to know about politics.
3. Our adversary, Russia, spent many millions on ads to get a Republican elected. Russia would be happy to see the USA fall apart. This tells you everything you need to know about politics.
4. Republicans repealed net neutrality (free internet), outlawed free-market pricing of Medicare drugs, and increased the deficit with enormous tax breaks for billionaires. These actions all move your money to the superbillionaires. This tells you everything you need to know about politics.

The Laws of Politics

1. Social conservatives are always on the wrong side of history.
2. The economy does better under Democrats than under Republicans.
3. Republicans put party ahead of country.
4. Republicans refuse to address the 30,000 annual gun deaths.
5. Republicans always put interests of the superwealthy ahead of the working class.
6. Conservatives delay progress but can never stop it.
7. Republicans continue repeating their lies long after they have been debunked.
8. Republicans, regardless of facts, never admit they are wrong or made a mistake.

Republicans Oppose Teaching Critical Thinking

A platform statement of the Texas Republican Party:
Knowledge-Based Education—
We oppose the teaching of Higher Order Thinking Skills (HOTS) (values clarification), critical thinking skills and similar programs that are simply a relabeling of Outcome-Based Education (OBE) (mastery learning) which focus on behavior modification and have the purpose of challenging the student's fixed beliefs and undermining parental authority.

Dictionary Definitions

Cognitive Dissonance

> In the field of psychology, cognitive dissonance is the mental discomfort experienced by a person who simultaneously holds two or more contradictory beliefs, ideas, or values.
>
> Sometimes people hold a core belief that is very strong. When they are presented with evidence that works against that belief, the new evidence cannot be accepted. It would create a feeling that is extremely uncomfortable called cognitive dissonance. And because it is so important to protect the core belief, they will rationalize, ignore and even deny anything that doesn't fit in with the core belief".
> —Frantz Fanon, famous psychiatrist

Dunning-Kruger Effect

> The Dunning-Kruger effect is a cognitive bias in which people of low ability have illusory superiority

and mistakenly assess their cognitive ability as greater than it is.

Liberal

[**lib**-er-*uh* l, **lib**-r*uh* l] adjective

1. Favorable to progress or reform, as in political or religious affairs.
2. Noting or pertaining to a political party advocating measures of progressive political reform.
3. Pertaining to, based on, or advocating liberalism, especially the freedom of the individual and government guarantees of individual rights and liberties.
4. Favorable to or in accord with concepts of maximum individual freedom possible, especially as guaranteed by law and secured by governmental protection of civil liberties.
5. Favoring or permitting freedom of action, especially with respect to matters of personal belief or expression: *a liberal policy toward dissident artists and writers.*
6. Relating to representational forms of government rather than aristocracies and monarchies.
7. Free from prejudice or bigotry, tolerant: *liberal attitude toward foreigners.*

Conservative

[k*uh* n-**sur**-v*uh*-tiv] adjective

1. Disposed to preserve existing conditions, institutions, etc., or to restore traditional ones, and to limit change.
2. Cautiously moderate or purposefully low: *a conservative estimate.*
3. Traditional in style or manner, avoiding novelty or showiness: *a conservative suit.*
4. Of or relating to the Conservative Party.
5. Having the power or tendency to conserve or preserve.

MAJOR ACCOMPLISHMENTS OF SOCIAL LIBERALS

- Women's right to vote
- Freedom to sell alcohol (after it was outlawed)
- Public education for everyone
- Fairness in broadcasting (1949–1987)
- Declaration of Independence from Britain
- Separation of church and state
- Child labor outlawed
- Emancipation Proclamation—end of slavery
- Medicare
- Freedom of same sex marriages
- Social Security
- Monopolies outlawed
- Freedom to use marijuana
- 1957 Civil Rights Act
- Affordable Care Act
- Worker-management agreements
  o Forty-hour workweek
  o Living wages
  o Employer health insurance
  o Work breaks
  o Extra pay for overtime hours
  o Equal opportunity for all races, genders, ethnicities
  o Protection from sexual harassment and inequality
  o Pension plans
  o Termination and discipline procedures
  o Paid vacations
  o Workers' rights
- Consumer protections from dangerous products
  o Safe food and drugs—FDA
  o Seat belts, catalytic converters, airbags
  o Potable water and breathable air—EPA
  o Consumer financial protections—CFPB

THE CONSERVATIVES' RECORD

- Slavery
- US Civil War (more dead than all other wars combined)
- Iraq War (weapons of mass destruction was a lie)
- Repealed Glass-Steagall limitations of bank speculations
- Voter suppression laws and gerrymandering
- Repealed fairness in broadcasting 1987
- Opposed independence from Great Britain
- Great Depression of 1929
- Great Recession of 2008
- Suppressed unions that made America great
- Filibustered/obstructed Obama's recovery and job bills
- Blocked health care for 70 years
- Refused to acknowledge the 30,000 annual gun deaths
- Refused to adjust minimum wage for inflation
- Refused to do anything about global warming
- Repealed Obama's net neutrality law
- Refused to fund cancer research

Republican Filibusters Blocking Obama Recovery Bills

- Creating American Jobs Act
- Ending Offshoring Act
- American Jobs Act
- First Responders Back to Work Act of 2011
- Repeal Big Oil Tax Subsidies Act
- The DREAM Act
- The DISCLOSE Act
- Employee Free Choice Act (EFCA)
- The public health care option
- Paycheck Fairness Act
- Permanent middle-class Bush tax cut extension
- Rescinding of the upper-income Bush tax cuts
- Public Safety Employer-Employee Cooperation Act
- Emergency Senior Citizens Relief Act
- The Buffett Rule

MAJOR REPUBLICAN LIES

- Saddam Hussein was behind 9/11.
- Democrats want everyone to have the same income.
- Iraq had weapons of mass destruction.
- There is no evidence of Russia's interference in our elections.
- Obama was elected by the people getting government handouts.
- All the world's scientists lied about global warming hoax.
- Hillary Clinton won the popular vote only by illegal aliens voting.
- Tax breaks for the wealthy would create jobs.
- If everyone carried guns there would be no gun killings
- Unions are communists.
- Democrats want unrestricted open borders.
- Adjusting the minimum wage for inflation would hurt the economy.
- Hillary Clinton is guilty of corruption.
- Obamacare was the worst thing the government has done.
- The Republican health-care plan was good for the working class.
- The Benghazi attack was caused by Hillary Clinton.
- The Clinton Foundation is a corrupt money-laundering front.

Chart 13
Happiness Rankings of Countries

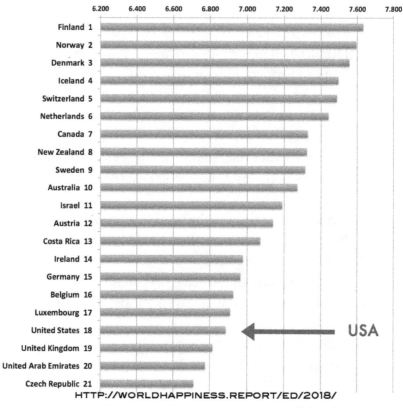

Chart 14
GINI Income Equality by Country

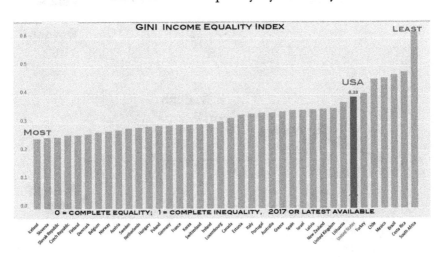

Source: http://www.indexmundi.com/facts/indicators/SI.POV.GINI/rankings

Chart 15
S&P 500 by President

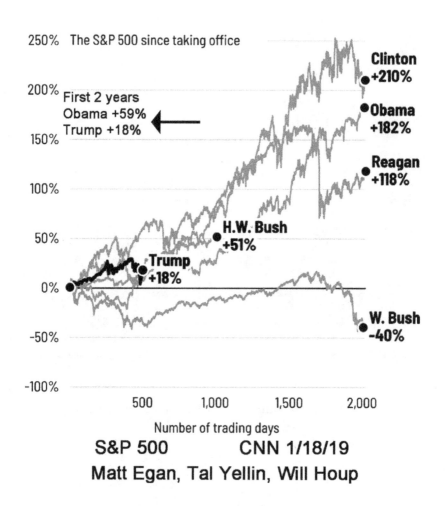

Source: http://presidentialdata.org;
https://www.forbes.com/sites/realspin/2016/11/07/trump-is-right-about-one-thing-the-economy-does-better-under-the-democrats/#6e8243cc6786

Chart 16

Indictments and Convictions by Administration

EXECUTIVE BRANCH CRIMINAL ACTIVITIES

	Criminal Indictments	Criminal Convictions	Prison Sentences
DEMOCRATS			
Obama	0	0	0
Clinton	2	1	1
Carter	1	0	0
Johnson	0	0	0
TOTAL	3	1	1
REPUBLICANS			
Trump	27+	5+	?
Bush 2	16	16	9
Bush 1	1	1	1
Reagan	26	16	8
Ford	1	1	1
Nixon	76	55	15
TOTAL	147	94	34

FAMOUS QUOTES BY TRUMP

"I came up with the phrase 'Prime the Pump' a couple of days ago. I thought it was good."
"I know words, I have the best words. I have the best."

"I have a good brain and I have said a lot of things."
"When you're a star, [women] let you do anything—grab them by the pussy."

After mimicking physical handicap of a reporter
"I did not mock that reporter."

On John McCain after five years in Vietnam POW camp
"I prefer soldiers who do not get captured."
    McCain remembered this and his vote stopped
    Trump's health care proposal.

Encouraging Russia to commit illegal political espionage
"Russia: I hope you're able to find the 30,000 emails that are missing."

After all US Intelligence agencies agree that Russia ran election ads
"President Putin said it's not Russia. I don't see any reason why it would be."

MUST-SEE REFERENCES

Videos

Chris Rock. [90].— an outstanding revelation on racism.
Jim Jefferies Part 1. [91].— humorous absurdities of gun control opposition.
Jim Jefferies Part 2. [92].

Books

Rosenthal, Elisabeth. *An American Sickness.*
    This book describes the many health-care schemes that put profits above service.
Conway, Erik M., and Naomi Oreskes. *Merchants of Doubt.*
    This book describes corporate schemes that put profits over consumer safety.

Chart 17
Federal Aid by State

Which States Rely Most on Federal Aid?
Federal Aid as a Percentage of State General Revenue (FY 2014)

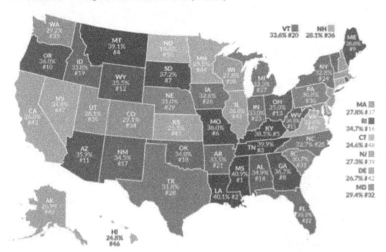

Notes: Figures are calculated by dividing each state's "Intergovernmental Revenue" by its "General Revenue." "General Revenue" includes all tax revenue but excludes utility revenue, liquor store revenue, and investment income from state pension funds. D.C. is designated as a local entity by the U.S. Census Bureau and thus not included here.

Source: U.S. Census Bureau; Tax Foundation

Federal Aid as a Percentage of State General Revenue

Lower — Higher

Chart 18
Gun-Death Rate

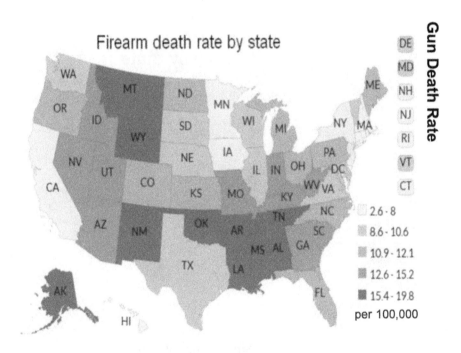

Source: https://fivethirtyeight.com/features/gun-deaths/

Chart 19
Obesity by State

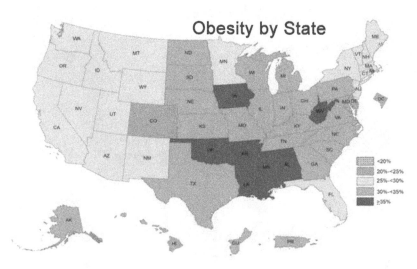

Source: Behavioral Risk Factor Surveillance System

Chart 20
Heart Failures by State

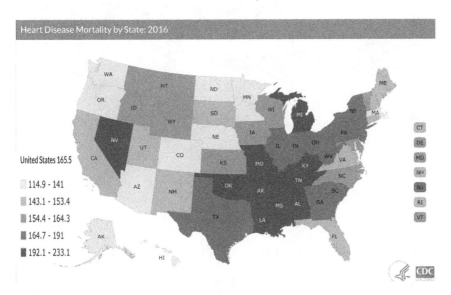

Source: Department of Health and Human Services, USA (CDC)

Chart 21
Median Household Income

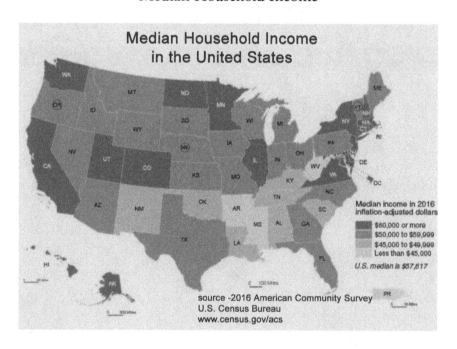

Source: 2016 American Community Survey US Census Bureau

REFERENCES

1. Limbaugh lies about Liberals
   https://www.adn.com/opinions/national-opinions/2018/12/25/liberals-and-conservatives-made-peace-at-this-university-but-rush-limbaugh-wasnt-buying-it/
2. Limbaugh lies about Liberals
   https://news.iheart.com/featured/rush-limbaugh/content/2018-05-07-rush-limbaugh-blog-yes-liberalism-must-be-defeated/
3. Dictionary Definitions
   http://www.dictionary.com
4. Psychological Differences
   https://www.businessinsider.com/psychological-differences-between-conservatives-and-liberals-2018-2
5. Your Political Beliefs Are Partly Shaped By Genetics
   http://blogs.discovermagazine.com/d-brief/2015/08/05/political-beliefs-genetic/#.W6raJi-ZPOY
6. Fox News controversies
   https://en.wikipedia.org/wiki/Fox_News_controversies#Content_analysis_studies
7. Watching Only Fox News Makes You Less Informed Than Watching No News At All
   https://www.businessinsider.com/study-watching-fox-news-makes-you-less-informed-than-watching-no-news-at-all-2012-5
8. Fox News misleading 72% of the time.
   https://en.wikipedia.org/wiki/Fox_News_controversies#Content_analysis_studies
9. Dunning-Krueger Effect
   https://en.wikipedia.org/wiki/Dunning–Kruger_effect
10. History of RF Transmission
    https://en.wikipedia.org/wiki/History_of_radio

11. Benefit of Clergy
    https://en.wikipedia.org/wiki/Benefit_of_clergy
12. Confederate Heroes Holidays
    https://www.texastribune.org/2018/01/19/some-texas-employees-get-today-celebrate-confederate-heroes/
13. Four black schoolgirls killed in Birmingham
    https://www.history.com/this-day-in-history/four-black-schoolgirls-killed-in-birmingham
14. NCAA 1963 Segregation in Basketball
    https://wtop.com/ncaa-basketball/2018/03/loyolas-run-shines-light-on-barrier-breaking-63-title-team/
15. Anti-Suffragist quotes
    https://www.rooshvforum.com/thread-20197.html
16. Bread and Roses Strike 1912
    https://revolutionaryworkers.org/the-1912-bread-and-roses-strike-lawrence-massachusetts/
17. Strikers shot by police
    https://en.wikipedia.org/wiki/Coal_strike_of_1902
18. Labor Laws
    https://www.afscme.org/news/publications/newsletters/works/november-december-1999/labors-top-10-accomplishments
19. Obamacare Approval
    https://www.kff.org/interactive/kaiser-health-tracking-poll-the-publics-views-on-the-aca/#?response=Favorable--Unfavorable&aRange=twoYear
20. Houston Sets Strict Rules for Robot Brothel
    https://www.houstonpublicmedia.org/articles/news/2018/10/03/306709/houston-sets-strict-rules-for-robot-brothel/
21. Should Prostitution be Legalized?
    http://maristpoll.marist.edu/531-should-prostitution-be-legalized/
22. College Students Using Sugar Daddies To Pay Off Loan Debt
    https://www.huffingtonpost.com/2011/07/29/seeking-arrangement-college-students_n_913373.html
23. 7 unspeakable words
    https://www.youtube.com/watch?v=vbZhpf3sQxQ
24. Cocaine Use Reduction
    https://drugabuse.com/library/drug-abuse-statistics/
25. Opioid Use Trend
    https://medmark.com/the-opioid-trend-in-the-millennial-generation/
26. Drugs in Portugal: Did Decriminalization Work?
    http://content.time.com/time/health/article/0,8599,1893946,00.html
    https://www.econlib.org/archives/2017/12/is_portugals_dr.html

27. Costs of Incarceration
    https://www.ocregister.com/2017/05/10/california-has-one-of-the-most-expensive-prison-systems-in-the-world/
28. Drugs And Crime Facts
    https://www.bjs.gov/content/dcf/correct.cfm
29. Medical expenses are the number one cause of bankruptcies
    https://www.huffingtonpost.com/simple-thrifty-living/top-10-reasons-people-go-_b_6887642.html
30. Billy Tauzin - Congressman and Lobbyist
    https://en.wikipedia.org/wiki/Billy_Tauzin
31. Medicare Prescription Drug Act
    https://en.wikipedia.org/wiki/Medicare_Prescription_Drug,_Improvement,_and_Modernization_Act
32. US drug prices compared to other countries
    https://www.exposingtruth.com/the-inhumanity-of-us-drug-prices-compared-to-other-countries/
33. Are CEOs Paid for Performance
    https://www.msci.com/www/research-paper/are-ceos-paid-for-performance-/0412607620
34. Highest Paid Health Care CEOs
    https://www.beckershospitalreview.com/rankings-and-ratings/18-of-the-highest-paid-ceos-in-healthcare.html
35. Senate panel votes down public option for health care bill
    http://www.cnn.com/2009/POLITICS/09/29/senate.public.option/
36. Comparative Performance of American Health Care
    https://www.commonwealthfund.org/publications/fund-reports/2007/may/mirror-mirror-wall-international-update-comparative-performance?redirect_source=/publications/fund-reports/2007/may/mirror--mirror-on-the-wall--an-international-update-on-the-comparative-performance-of-american-healt
37. 1,200 Children Murdered by Guns Since 2018 Parkland Massacre
    https://www.thedailybeast.com/nearly-1200-us-kids-dead-from-guns-since-parkland-massacre-report
38. Republican Senators Against Background Checks
    http://www.motherjones.com/politics/2013/04/number-senators-voted-against-background-checks-proposal/
39. Brown Bess musket
    https://en.wikipedia.org/wiki/Brown_Bess
40. GDP Growth by Party
    http://fortune.com/2014/07/29/economic-growth-democratic-presidents/
41. Presidents and the U.S. Economy: An Econometric Exploration

http://www.nber.org/papers/w20324?utm_campaign=ntw&utm_medium=email&utm_source=ntw; http://presidentialdata.org
42. Presidential Economy Data
http://presidentialdata.org;
https://www.forbes.com/sites/realspin/2016/11/07/trump-is-right-about-one-thing-the-economy-does-better-under-the-democrats/#6e8243cc6786
43. Tranches and Mortgage Backed Securities.
https://www.thebalance.com/tranches-definition-risks-and-how-they-work-3305901
44. Derivatives and Mortgage Backed Securities
https://www.thebalance.com/role-of-derivatives-in-creating-mortgage-crisis-3970477
45. Credit Default Swaps.
https://corporatefinanceinstitute.com/resources/knowledge/finance/credit-default-swap-cds/
46. Tulip Mania
https://en.wikipedia.org/wiki/Tulip_mania
47. GINI Index - Country Ranking
http://www.indexmundi.com/facts/indicators/SI.POV.GINI/rankings
48. Why Sam Brownback's Tax Cuts failed to make Kansas thrive
http://www.chicagotribune.com/news/opinion/commentary/ct-kansas-sam-brownback-tax-cuts-20170321-story.html
49. Real State Growth
http://www.usgovernmentdebt.us/compare_state_debt
50. Per capita Real GDP of the United States in 2017 by State
http://www.statista.com/statistics/248063/per-capita-us-real-gross-domestic-product-gdp-by-state/
51. Here's where dissatisfied teachers are taking action next
https://www.cnn.com/2018/04/25/us/teacher-walkouts-and-rallies-arizona-colorado-north-carolina-utah/index.html
52. Projected National Debt
https://www.latimes.com/politics/la-na-pol-tax-cuts-debt-20180626-story.html
53. Why the Gap Between Worker Pay and Productivity Is So Problematic
https://www.theatlantic.com/business/archive/2015/02/why-the-gap-between-worker-pay-and-productivity-is-so-problematic/385931/
54. Labor Unions in the United States
https://en.wikipedia.org/wiki/Labor_unions_in_the_United_States
55. Different Types of Pregnancy Loss
https://www.verywell.com/types-of-pregnancy-loss-2371413
56. Lead Action News
http://www.lead.org.au/lanv8n1/l8v1-3.html

57. Ford Pinto
https://en.wikipedia.org/wiki/Ford_Pinto
58. Polonium
https://en.wikipedia.org/wiki/Polonium ppm
59. Contesting the Science of Smoking
https://www.theatlantic.com/politics/archive/2016/05/low-tar-cigarettes/481116/
60. 97% of scientist today believe global warming is man made.
https://www.ucsusa.org/global-warming/science-and-impacts/science/scientists-agree-global-warming-happening-humans-primary-cause#.W88wRi_MzOY
61. 10 climate change villains
https://www.cnn.com/2015/08/13/opinions/gallery/top-climate-change-contributors/index.html
62. Global Warming Denial Questions Answered
https://skepticalscience.com/argument.php?f=percentage
63. Amazing video of CO_2 Accumulation Over Time
https://www.youtube.com/watch?v=UatUDnFmNTY
64. US Cities, States, and Businesses Vow to Meet Paris Climate Commitments
https://insideclimatenews.org/news/05062017/paris-climate-agreement-trump-bloomberg-cities-states-businesses
65. 10,000 lies: another Trump milestone
https://www.bostonglobe.com/opinion/2019/05/03/lies-another-trump-milestone/am67Gm7MAeojoupEM8aAXN/story.html?p1=Article_Inline_Text_Link
66. Cognitive Dissonance
https://en.wikipedia.org/wiki/Cognitive_dissonance
67. Why are Conservatives More Susceptible to Believing Lies
http://www.slate.com/articles/health_and_science/science/2017/11/why_conservatives_are_more_susceptible_to_believing_in_lies.html
68. GOP's Voter Suppression Tactics
https://www.truthdig.com/articles/data-suppression-is-the-gops-latest-anti-voter-tactic-for-the-midterms/
69. Polling Places Remain a Target Ahead of November Elections
https://www.pewtrusts.org/en/research-and-analysis/blogs/stateline/2018/09/04/polling-places-remain-a-target-ahead-of-november-elections
70. Clinton Foundation rating
https://www.charitynavigator.org/index.cfm?bay=search.summary&orgid=16680
71. Trump Foundation to Close

https://www.cbsnews.com/news/trump-foundation-shutting-down-amid-allegations-by-ny-attorney-general-money-used-for-personal-benefit/
72. 7 Benghazi probes so far (plus one incomplete)
https://www.politifact.com/truth-o-meter/statements/2015/oct/12/hillary-clinton/clinton-there-have-been-7-benghazi-probes-so-far/
73. The $20 Trillion U.S. Debt: Which President Contributed the Most
https://www.debtconsolidation.com/us-debt-presidents/
74. US Image Suffers as Publics Around the World Question Trump's Leadership
http://www.pewglobal.org/2017/06/26/u-s-image-suffers-as-publics-around-world-question-trumps-leadership/
75. 83% of voters support keeping FCC's net neutrality rules
http://thehill.com/policy/technology/364528-poll-83-percent-of-voters-support-keeping-fccs-net-neutrality-rules
76. Kellyanne Conway refuses to answer hardball question
https://www.youtube.com/watch?v=VSrEEDQgFc8
77. Johnny Carson as Carnac the Magnificent
https://www.youtube.com/watch?v=ZFQFf_Vb0Hw
78. Texas GOP rejects 'critical thinking' skills.
https://www.washingtonpost.com/blogs/answer-sheet/post/texas-gop-rejects-critical-thinking-skills-really/2012/07/08/gJQAHNpFXW_blog.html?noredirect=on&utm_term=.b864f6897c9d
79. Stephen Colbert on GOP suppression of critical thinking
http://www.cc.com/video-clips/577ry9/the-colbert-report-the-word---on-the-straight---narrow-minded
80. Bill Maher - Republicans refuse to stop repeating proven lies
https://www.youtube.com/watch?v=gb07hYEo_XI
81. Hourly Earnings of Uber And Taxi Drivers
https://www.forbes.com/sites/niallmccarthy/ 2016/11/28/fare-deal-how-the-hourly-earnings-of-uber-and-taxi-drivers-measure-up-infographic/#18a3f88b689a
82. Projected Life Expectancies
http://www.ipss.go.jp/index-e.asp
83. The GOP's no-compromise pledge
https://www.politico.com/story/2010/10/the-gops-no-compromise-pledge-044311
84. Hate crimes increased by 17 percent
https://www.vox.com/policy-and-politics/2018/11/13/18091646/fbi-hate-crimes-2017
85. Your Political Beliefs Are Partly Shaped By Genetics
http://blogs.discovermagazine.com/d-brief/2015/08/05/political-beliefs-genetic/#.W6raJi-ZPOY

86. Asch conformity experiments
    https://en.wikipedia.org/wiki/Asch_conformity_experiments
87. Texas secession movement
    https://en.wikipedia.org/wiki/Texas_secession_movements
88. Yes California
    https://en.wikipedia.org/wiki/Yes_California
89. Citizens United
    https://en.wikipedia.org/wiki/Citizens_United_v._FEC
90. Chris Rock
    https://www.youtube.com/watch?v=f3PJF0YE-x4 -
91. Jim Jefferies Part 1
    https://www.youtube.com/watch?v=0rR9IaXH1M0 -
92. Jim Jefferies Part 2
    https://www.youtube.com/watch?v=a9UFyNy-rw4 -

INDEX

A

Abigail (wife of David), 16
Abital (wife of David), 16
abolition, 33, 36–37
Abortion, 95
acid rain, 103
Acropolis, 16
acts of God, 96–97
Adams, John, 27
Adventures of Ozzie and Harriet, The, 91
Advisory Commission on Election Integrity, 118
aerodynamics, 104
African American, 27
Africans, 30–31
Age of Enlightenment, 23
agriculture, 20
Ahinoam (wife of David), 16
Alabama, 31, 36
Alan Binder, 74
Alexander Hamilton, 37
Alex Jones, 139
Allen Greenspan, 79
alternative facts, 124
American Indian, 81
American Medical Association, 41
American Revolution, 26

Americans, 6, 27–29, 32, 35–36, 38, 42, 46, 50, 54, 56, 64–68, 71, 80, 99, 107, 113, 117–18, 120, 137
American Sickness, An (Elisabeth Rosenthal), 66
anarchists, 21
Ancient Democracies, 14, 17
anesthesiologists, 60
Anglo-French War, 29
Annie LoPizzo, 39
Anthony, Susan, 38
Anthony Giuseppe, 40
antibiotics, 35
antislavery, 31, 34
Apple, 89, 129
arabic, 21
Arizona, 88
Arnold, Benedict, 29
Articles of Secession, 33–34
Aryan master race, 50
assemblies, 17
Athenian, 15–16
Australia, 119
automation, 130

B

bacillus Calmette-Guerin (BCG), 66
background checks, 41, 68, 80, 113

bangers and mash, 56
bankruptcies, 59–60
Barcelona, 56
Bathsheba (wife of David), 16
Bear Bryant, 36
Beddall, Joseph, 40
Benefit of Clergy, 27
Benghazi, 121–22
Benjamin Franklin, 29
Bible, 138
Bill Clinton, 41
Bill Maher, 125
Billy Tauzin, 60–61
Black Death, 130
Bloomberg, 87
Boston, 27–28
Boston Massacre, 27
British, 2, 21, 27–30
British Museum, 21
Brownback, 87
Brown Bess, 71
Brownsville, Pennsylvania, 40
buprenorphine, 48
Bureau of Justice Statistics, 48
Bush, George W., 79

C

Caesar, Julius, 14, 17
calculator, 21
California, 15, 36, 49, 81, 88, 123, 135
Caltech, 115
Canada, 27, 29, 47, 59, 61, 103
cancer, 101
cannabis, 46
capitalism, 78, 81, 83–86
Capricorn, 107
Caribbean Islands, 29, 31
Carlin, George, 45
Carson, Johnny, 125
catalytic converters, 103
Catholic, 23

Catholics, 37
Cato, 48
caveman, 14
Celsius, 53–54
Center for Public Integrity, 62
Center for Responsive Politics, 62
Central America, 47, 49
CFPB (Consumer Financial Protection Bureau), 41, 80–81
Charles I, 18
Charles II, 18
Chicago, 31
China, 21, 56, 81, 85
Chris Matthews, 74
Christ, 16
Christian, 23, 37
Christianity, 21
Christians, 16
Chronicles 3:1-3, 16
CIA, 121
Cigarette Cancer, 101
Cincinnati Red Stockings, 59
Citizen, 18
Citizens United, 138
city-state, 15, 17
Civil War, 27, 33–36, 137
Clean Air Act, 103
Cleisthenes, 15
climate scientists, 104
Clinton, Hillary, 121–22
Clinton Foundation, 121
CNN, 9, 111
CO_2, 102, 105–7
cocaine, 47–48
cognitive dissonance, 116
Columbus, 51
communications, 19, 22
communism, 81, 84
concussions, 58
confederacy, 33
Confederate, 33

conservative, 1–2, 7, 13–14, 24, 26, 28, 30, 32, 36–37, 39, 43, 51, 53, 64, 67, 79, 97, 108, 117–18, 136
conservatives, 2–3, 6–7, 24, 26, 28, 30, 32, 35–37, 39–41, 43–44, 46, 96, 130, 137
Constitution, 37–38, 123, 137
consuls, 17
Continental Army, 29–30
Continental Congress, 37
Convention on Climate Change, 107
Conway, Erik M., 102
   Masters of Deceit, 102
Conway, Kellyanne, 124–25
cost of living, 91
Council of the Plebs, 17
Craig's List, 60
Crispus Attucks, 27
critical thinking, 125
critical thinking skills, 125
Cromwell, Oliver, 18
crusade, 33

D

daddy, sugar, 44, 59
Dark Ages, 17
David, 16
David (biblical character), 16
Death Panels, 41–42
decimal, 13, 21, 52
deficits, 73
democracy, 36
Democrats, 32, 39, 41, 61–62, 73, 75, 78, 80, 87, 90, 111–17, 123, 126, 134, 139
demokratia, 15
deregulation, 79
derivatives, 79
dictators, 14, 19, 23
dikasteria, 15
Diocletian, 17

divorce, 46
Dixiecrats, 32
DNA, 95, 97, 116, 129, 135
dockworkers, 128
Dodd-Frank, 80
DRD4 (dopamine receptor D4), 2
drug clinic, 49
Dubner, Stephen, 130
   Freakonomics, 130
Dunning-Kruger Effect, 12
Durham, William, 40

E

Earth, 13, 98
East Africa, 13
eastern empire, 17
Eglah (wife of David), 16
ekklesia, 15
Election Day, 118
Elizabeth Stanton, 38
Emoluments, 123
encyclopedias, 128
England, 30, 55, 59, 66
English, 1–2, 18–20, 45, 86, 97
EPA, 99
Equator, 52
Ethiopia, 13
Europe, 17, 21–22, 24, 71
evolution, 18, 22
Exceptionalism, 50, 53, 55, 59, 66
extramarital sex, 16

F

Fahrenheit, 53–54
Fair Labor Standards Act, 40
fairness doctrine, 7–8, 12
fairness in broadcasting, 120, 138–39
fairness regulation, 8
fake news, 116, 124
fallopian tube, 95
family values, 124

FBI, 31
Federal Government, 33
Federal Reserve, 79, 81
Fibonacci, Leonardo, 21
   Liber Abaci, 21
field of genopolitical research, 135
Fifteenth Amendment, 35
First Amendment, 7
fiscal conservative, 79
fluoridated water, 103
football, 56–58
Force Out Rule, 59
Ford, Gerald, 41
Ford, Henry, 90
Ford Pinto, 99–100
Fortune (magazine), 74
Fortune 500, 108
Fourteenth Amendment, 35
401K, 91
Fox, Justin, 87
Fox News, 8, 12, 107, 116, 119, 139
FOXP2, 20
France, 27, 29–30, 85
Freakonomics (Levitt and Dubner), 130
French, 27, 30–31, 52
Führer, 6

G

gas chambers, 6
gay, 41
GDP, 74–75, 88, 129
geology, 104
George III, 28
Georgia, 31, 34
German invaders, 30
German mercenaries, 29
Germany, 6, 22, 65–66, 85
gerrymandering, 36
Glass-Steagall Act, 78–80
Global Warming, 103–4
God, 16, 96–98

Golden Age, 16
Golden Valley Lending, 81
Government Accountability Office, 64
government insurance option, 65
GPS (global posistioning system), 25
gram, 52
Great Britain, 29
Great Hoax, 104
Great Recession, 78–80, 84, 88, 119, 149
Greece, 14–16
Greeks, 16
Greenwald, Glenn, 48
Gutenberg, Johannes, 22
Gutenberg Bible, 22

H

Haggith (wife of David), 16
Harvey (hurricane), 106
health care, 41, 59–60
Health-care, 64
Health Care, 59, 65
heroin, 48
Hertz, Heinrich, 24
Hertzian waves, 24
Hitler, Adolf, 6, 127
HIV, 48
HMOs, 60
Hollywood, 7
hominids, 13
Homo sapiens, 13, 20, 51
Hooters, 104
Hoover, J. Edgar, 31
house, 41, 60, 80
House Committee on Energy and Commerce, 60
human, 19–20, 22, 31, 43, 46, 95–98, 100–102, 105, 127–29
human nature, 46
hunchbacks, 54–55
Hutchinson, Thomas, 27
hydrodynamics, 104

I

Iacocca, Lee, 100
Illegal Drugs, 46
Illinois, 31
imperial, 52–53
imperial system, 51–52
incomes, 74
independence, 26
India, 21, 85
industrial accidents, 39
inflation, 90
Iraqi, 111
Irma (hurricane), 106
Italian, 21, 97
Italy, 48, 54, 85

J

Japan, 21
Jedi, 112
Jerusalem, 16
Jesus Christ, 16
Jews, 37
Jim Crow laws, 35
jobs, 74
Jones, Alex, 8, 139
justice, 19
Justice Department, 102

K

Kansas, 87–88
Kentucky, 88
kilometer, 52
Kilroy, Matthew, 27
Ku Klux Klan, 112

L

language, 20
Latin, 21, 51
Lawrence, Massachusetts, 39
lead-210, 101
Lee, Robert E., 34
Lehman Brothers Holdings Inc., 79
Leo X (pope), 23
Leviticus 20:10, 16
Levitt, Steven, 130
   Freakonomics, 130
Lexington, 28
Liber Abaci (Leonardo Fibonacci), 21
liberal, 1–3, 13–14, 16, 18–19, 22–24,
   26–28, 31–32, 36–37, 39, 117
Liberalism, 19
liberals, 6, 12, 27, 31, 46
libertarian, 14
Libertarians, 44
liberties, 18–19
life expectancy, 129
Limbaugh, Rush, xx, 7–8
Limonada, 49
lobbyists, 60, 62
Lombardi Trophy, 58
London, 29, 58
longshoremen, 128
Louisiana, 31, 60
loyalists, 28–29
Loyola, 36
LVN, 60

M

Maacah (wife of David), 16
macroeconomic metrics., 74
magistrates, 17
Magna Carta, 18
manga comics, 21
Marconi, Guglielmo, 24
marijuana, 46–48
marriage, 16, 41
Mars, 53
Martin, Lockheed, 53
Massachusetts, 27–28, 59
Masters of Deceit (Oreskes and
   Conway), 102

mathematics, 21, 86, 104
Maxwell, James Clerk, 24
McCarthy, Joe, 7–8
McDonald's, 88
Medical Billing and Coding, 64
Medicare Drug Bill, 60
Medicare Prescription Drug, Improvement, and Modernization Act, 61
Mediterranean, 17
Mencken, H. L., 73
Messi, Lionel, 56
meters, 52
methadone, 48
methamphetamine, 48
metric, 48, 52–53
Mexico, 47–48, 58, 85
Mexico City, 58
Michal (wife of David), 16
migration, 20
mile, 51–52
military budgets, 126
Millennials, 25
mille passus, 51
minimum wage, 90
Mississippi, 31, 36
monarchies, 19, 24, 136
monogamous, 23
monopolies, 85
Montgomery, Hugh, 27
Mormon, 23
Mormons, 23
Morris, Philip, 102
MSNBC, 9
Mulvaney, Mick, 80
mutations, 20

N

Naismith, James, 59
NASA, 53
National Bureau of Economic Research, 74
national debt, 88–89
National Health Care, 41–42
National Highway Traffic Safety Administration (NHTSA), 100
Nazi, 6
NBC, 7, 12
NCAA, 36
Neanderthals, 14
negro, 33
net neutrality, 41, 113, 123
Nevada, 43
New Jersey, 29
New York, 23, 38, 59, 124, 129
Nineteenth Amendment, 38–39
Nixon, Richard, 47
NO2, 103
North Atlantic Current, 51
North Carolina, 30
North Korean, 119
North Pole, 52, 105

O

Obama, Barack, 41, 111
Obamacare, 41–42, 65
Oklahoma, 88
Old Testament, 16
Oneida Community, 23
onion market, 84
onions, 84
opioids, 47
Order of Saint Augustine, 22
Oreskes, Naomi, 102, 159
  Masters of Deceit, 102
ovum, 95
ozone depletion, 103

P

Palin, Sarah, 124
parliament, 18, 27–28

Parthenon, 16
patriots, 28–29
Paul of Tarsus, 16
Pax Romana, 21
Pennsylvania, 135
Pericles, 16
Persian, 15
Peter the Great, 14
Pharmaceutical Research and Manufacturers of America, 62
Philip (prince), 127
Philip Morris, 102
physics, 104
Physiological, 2
pictographs, 21
Pinto (car model), 100–101
Pirro, Jeanine, 12
plebeians, 17
plebs, 17
Pliocene, 107
polonium-210, 101
polygamy, 16, 23
population, 130
pornography, 44
Portugal, 47–48
Portuguese, 31, 48
premarital sex, 46
profits, 74
Project on Excellence in Journalism, 9
prostitution, 43–45
Protestant Reformation, 22
Psalm 51, 27
Public Option, 65
Pursuit of Happiness, 51

Q

quadratic, 21
Quakers, 37

R

racism, 35–36

radio, 22, 138
radium-226, 101
radon-222, 101
Reefer Madness, 46
republic, 17
Republican, 7, 31–32, 34, 41–42, 60–61, 73–75, 78–81, 87–90, 111–14, 116–17, 119–20, 123, 125, 139
Republican Party, 31–32, 34, 89
Republicans, 32
Revolutionary War, 28, 30
RFP, 60
right amygdala, 2
Ripon, Wisconsin, 31
Roe v. Wade, 97
Roman, 17–19, 21, 51
Roman Empire, 17, 21
Romanian, 2
roman numerals, 20
Roman Republic, 18
Romans, 16, 18, 20
Rome, 16–17, 20, 56
Roosevelt, Franklin Delano, 16, 40
Rosenthal, Elisabeth, *An American Sickness*, 66, 159
Rosetta Stone, 21
Russia, 111
Russian Main Intelligence Directorate, 119

S

Samuel 3:2-5, 16
San Francisco, 129
Saratoga, New York, 29
secession, 33, 137
Second Amendment, 71
secondhand smoke, 103
segregation, 35
Senate, 7, 17, 41, 79, 167
senators, 15, 17, 167
Seneca Falls, 38

sex, 23–24, 31, 43–46, 138
sexual incompatibility, 46
Shang dynasty, 18
slavery, xix, 5, 27, 30–33, 35, 37, 147, 149
Slavery, 30–33, 35, 37
smartphone, 21
Smartphone apps, 128
SO2, 103
Soccer, 56
social conservatives, 13, 26, 35–38, 41–43, 45, 103
socialism-capitalism, 81
social progress, 141
Social Security, 59, 81
South America, 24
South Carolina, 30
Spain, 48, 61
Spanish, 31
spermatozoon, 95
Springfield, Massachusetts, 59
Stamp Act, 27
statistics, 104
Stone Age, 21
Sugar Act, 27
sunspots, 106
Super Bowl, 21
Supply Side, 86–87
Supreme Court, 36, 42, 97, 138
SUV, 80
Swarthmore College, 135
swastika, 50
Sweden, 85, 103

T

Tanzania, 14
Tea Act, 27–28
tectonics, 104
temperature, 53
Tennessee, 31, 38
Texas, 31, 33, 137, 144
thermodynamics, 104

Thirteenth Amendment, 35
Time, 54
traitors, 30
Trickle Down, 86–87
Tropics of Cancer, 107
Truman, Harry, 41
Tulip Bulb Mania, 84
TV, 1, 12, 45, 91, 107, 136, 138

U

UN, 107
unemployment, 74
Unions, 91
United States of America, 34, 102
universal health care, 41, 60, 65–66, 81
Uranium One, 120–21
US, 3, 7, 35, 44, 51–52, 54–56, 59–62, 64–67, 83, 85, 103, 107, 123, 134–35, 137–38
USC, 36
US Constitution, 7
US military, 108

V

VA, 60
veto, 18
Vietnam War, 35
Virginia, 31
Voter Fraud, 117
Voting Rights Act, 36

W

Wallace, George, 31
Walmart, 88
War on Drugs, 47
Watson, Mark, 74
western empire, 17
West Virginia, 88
White House, 21, 73, 75
women voting, 37
Working Class, 40, 91

World War I, 35
World War II, 6, 35, 89, 91
Writing, 20–21

Y

Yankees, 32
Yellow Pages, 128
Yorktown, Virginia, 30
YouTube, 95

Z

Zombie Lies, 125
zygote, 95–97